MEMORIES OF THE

Cornish Fishing Industry

Sheila Bird

D1447199

COUNTRYSIDE BOOKS
NEWBURY BERKSHIRE

First published 2010
© Sheila Bird 2010

COUNTRYSIDE BOOKS
3 Catherine Road
Newbury, Berkshire

To view our complete range of books,
please visit us at
www.countrysidebooks.co.uk

ISBN 978 1 84674 157 9

Cover picture of Mevagissey harbour,
courtesy of Mevagissey Museum

Designed by Peter Davies, Nautilus Design

Produced through MRM Associates Ltd., Reading
Typeset by CJWT Solutions, St Helens
Printed by Information Press, Oxford

Contents

Dedication

*To all the Cornish fishermen
lost at sea*

Introduction

Fishing has been a way of life around the wild and windswept Cornish coast for centuries, for fish was the staple diet of the hardy folk who colonised this south-western peninsula jutting out into the stormy Atlantic Ocean.

In early times a variety of small craft designed to cope with local conditions would put to sea from every little cove and inlet along this long, indented coastline which offered some degree of shelter and scope to haul their boats ashore above the high tide mark. Initially, the seafaring population would have dwelt in small hutted settlements close to the shore, with basic timber structures alongside their boats to store their fishing equipment.

As time went by, protective quays were established in the more favourable locations, which were usually at the head of a bay on river estuaries. More substantial buildings constructed of stone or cob began to proliferate around these workaday harbours, progressing up the hillsides as needs dictated. They incorporated easily accessible fish stores and fish cellars at the lower level, with very basic accommodation for fishermen and their families above. Ports such as Polperro, Mevagissey, Mousehole, St Ives and Port Isaac are pleasing reminders of those early days.

The fishermen of Cornwall have long enjoyed a special bond of friendship and rivalry with their counterparts across the water, with those on the Channel coast ideally positioned to indulge in 'free trading' activities with Guernsey and Roscoff. The stretch of coastline between Plymouth and Polperro was the scene of smuggling exploits in the early 18th century, with the men of Cawsand Bay enjoying a particularly enviable reputation for their seamanship and daring. In 2005 some fishermen tending their boats at Portwrinkle, where the master smuggler Thomas

The fishermen of old lived above fish cellars, where they stored their equipment. (Sheila Bird Collection)

Helman's cottage remains, were keen to tell me that the wide expanse of Whitsand Bay was a much favoured place for the landing and concealment of illicit consignments. 'See, they could hide the kegs among the rocks and undergrowth along the cliffs,' said one. 'Then they was taken up to Craft'ole and inland through the quiet narrow lanes.'

If the Cornish fishermen enjoyed a certain notoriety on this account, they were also acknowledged for their bravery in carrying out spontaneous rescues in their own boats, and for serving as crewmen after the Royal National Lifeboat Institution established lifeboat stations all around the Cornish coast.

As early as the 1520s West Country fishermen were braving the stormy Atlantic to engage in the prestigious Newfoundland trade, generally regarded as the most exacting of all sea enterprises. In the early 17th century the ports of Saltash, Looe, Fowey, Mevagissey, St Mawes, Falmouth, St Keverne, Penzance, St Ives and Padstow were all taking part in this great adventure, which involved being away for about 18 months and required tremendous endurance. The Cornish link with Newfoundland's fisheries extended into the 19th century.

The fishing industry had gained momentum during the 17th and 18th centuries, when Fowey, Falmouth, Penzance and St Ives established themselves as the principal ports. By the mid-19th century the St Ives pilchard fishery was the largest in the world, with 249 seines in the port. The St Ives men were also engaged in fishing for mackerel, as well as for herring off the Irish coast.

Fishing endeavour had long generated employment for a number of spin-off trades on the shore. For apart from the men, women and children who washed, cleaned and processed the fish on the quayside, others would be engaged in boatbuilding and making ropes, nets, crab-pots, casks and other equipment. Cargoes of fish provided additional freight for shipping, and later on for the railways, thus opening up new markets. Nothing was ever wasted. Surplus oil from the processing of fish was sold as fuel, and anything left over went as fertiliser on the land.

More intensive fishing in these waters by local and itinerant

Carrying out maintenance work on a fishing boat at Port Isaac in April 1947. (George Ellis Collection, Cornish Studies Library)

fishermen in the 19th century led to diminishing fish stocks, and hardship in the coastal communities when the fishing failed.

The need to protect our marine environment and take measures to allow fish stocks to replenish themselves had been recognised by this time, and in the late 1800s various Acts of Parliament and restrictions on fishing activities in this area were emplaced. This was a tremendous blow to the fisherfolk, many of whom had invested their life savings in expensive boats and equipment. They felt that their lives were being ruined by bureaucrats who knew little or nothing about localised coastal conditions, fishing or the breeding habits of the species concerned.

The 20th century saw an increasing number of more sophisticated British and foreign fishing vessels in our waters, capable of netting vast quantities of fish. This again led to the depletion of our fish stocks, more rules and regulations, and incentives for our fishermen to lay up their boats. At the beginning of the 21st century, Newlyn and Looe have emerged as our premier fishing ports.

Fishing has, therefore, been a complete way of life for centuries in Cornwall, where sons followed fathers and grandfathers in the family boats. Their love of the sea was such that they took to their boats for pleasure too, becoming deadly rivals at the very popular regattas, and the best of mates in the pub afterwards.

This book follows the fortunes of Cornish fishermen through war and peace, through good times and bad. In writing it I have drawn on interviews carried out with those fishermen over the last 28 years, and feel very privileged to have known such wonderful people.

Sheila Bird

Acknowledgements

I would like to extend a big thank you to the Cornish Studies Library at Redruth, for their help and to everyone else who has contributed to the making of this book.

Chapter 1

Traditional Fishing and Fishing Craft

'Lord, spare our labour, and send them in with a blessing. Amen.'
(Prayer traditionally said by the fishermen as they
consigned their nets to the deep)

In former times Cornwall was renowned for its pilchard fishing. These migratory fish, colloquially known as the 'gypsy herring' on account of their resemblance to the larger species, appeared in gigantic shoals off the Cornish coast around the end of July/ beginning of August, pursued by predators such as dogfish, hake, cod, and flocks of sea birds. This massive army of fish created an amazing spectacle as they passed Land's End, where some veered to the north-east, while the bulk proceeded along the Channel coast as far as Bigbury Bay and Start Point.

Look-out men called 'huers' were stationed on the cliffs to

watch for signs of approaching shoals, which created a red tinge in the water. As soon as they beheld this welcome sight, they would shout 'Hevva! Hevva! Hevva!', whereupon the local inhabitants rushed down to the shore and put to sea in pursuit. Their course was directed by the huers, making semaphore-like signals with furze bushes.

The seine fishery was designed specifically for enclosing shoals of pilchards in enormous nets (or seines). Three boats took part in the operation, under the guidance of the Master Seiner. When the net was full, but not overloaded, the seine was drawn into shallower waters, where extra hands assisted in 'tucking' it. This involved gathering it up and transferring the catch into smaller boats. The fish were then taken ashore to be cured and packed into hogshead casks before being exported to Italy and Spain. The seines operated between sunrise and sunset, and early tourists were captivated by this picturesque workaday hive of industry.

Drift net fishing, geared to mackerel as well as pilchards, took place between sunset and sunrise several miles from the shore. A

An early tourist in stylish gear is intrigued by the workaday scene of taking the pilchards ashore at Sennen Cove in the early 20th century. (Cornish Studies Library)

Oyster dredging in Falmouth harbour in the early 1900s.
(Sheila Bird Collection)

string of nets 30 ft deep, and strung out a mile or so, drifted with the tide so as to intercept and entangle the fish by their gills. A mid-19th century guidebook enthused: 'The principal entertainment afforded by the drift fishing to the stranger is the daily recurring spectacle of the little fleet on the wing, its red sails all a-flame in the beams of the setting sun.'

Fish living at deeper levels were caught by hook and line. Crabs, lobsters and crayfish were captured in baited wicker pots closer to the shore, while salmon and oyster fishing were carried out in the wide river estuaries.

Oyster dredging is thought to have been a way of life in the Fal and Truro rivers since Roman times, and is still being practised in the traditional way, without the use of engines. The distinctive shallow-draught boats, rigged as gaff cutters with long bowsprits, evolved over the centuries. They were originally known as the Truro River Boats, and were something akin to the Falmouth

Quay Punts, but they are now referred to as the Falmouth Working Boats.

The oysters spawned in summer and the oyster dredgers worked from October to March, under licence. The dredges resembled netted bags, held open with a rigid framework, which were dragged slowly along the bed of the river. A boat with two men aboard was capable of towing four or five dredges, but the operation had to be carried out slowly, to prevent them being lifted from the bottom. The sails of the boat were set to allow her to drift slowly, and the nets hauled in carefully to avoid tangling. An oyster bailiff went around with a brass ring having an inside measurement of two and five-eighths inches; oysters smaller than this were to be returned to the water to allow them to mature.

Salmon fishing is another traditional living. Robert Chapman, now fishing out of Looe, told me of his early days on the river Lynher:

'Father was a salmon fisherman on the river, and I started from a small place called Antony Passage, with my brothers. We started salmon fishing at first, and then we progressed to put to sea, catching lobsters.

'We had a 16-ft rowing boat, just made for salmon fishing. It's done with a seine net. You shoot the net in a semi-circle, and in the centre of the net there's what you call a bunt, which is a bit of a cod end – without the cod end, if you know what I mean! It's just a bag – a cavity – in the net.

'So you encircle the fish and the fish go in the net. Then you'd draw the net on the mud bank. The fish would run back into the bunt, and then you'd have it captured. It's done with just one boat and we used to do it with four hands. But when the nylon net replaced the heavy old cotton ones, we could manage with two. That was in the 1960s.

'The season ran from March till the end of August, so you needed to find work between the other months. We wanted to be full-time fishermen, so then we progressed to

Newquay luggers setting off for the fishing grounds around 1905.
(Cornish Studies Library)

lobster fishing, and bought a bigger boat called *Our Boys*, which was an old Looe lugger. Then we moved to Looe and went crab fishing in summer and mackerel fishing in the winter, with long-lining for conger eels, and rays and things. The boat we've got now is the *John Wesley*. My son is the skipper of the *John Wesley* and I work the smaller boat called the *Mordros*.'

The old seine boats and the bigger boats were owned by merchants or a consortium of fishermen, whereas many of the independently minded fishermen aspired to owning and operating their own small craft. Old-timer Henry Johns of Mevagissey remarked: 'In my day you would have a few pounds, and you would borrow some from a relative fer simply to have a boat, and work her off, see? But now 'tis that much money with all the electronics they got in the wheelhouse and that, they got to have a grant from the government!'

Chapter 2

Learning by Experience

Not every fisherman came from a fishing family. Claudie Richards of Polruan had a somewhat unorthodox boyhood introduction to the waterfront after the First World War, which serves to demonstrate the value of learning by experience.

As we were yarning away in his home overlooking the harbour from the Fowey side, one day in the 1990s, he explained to me that an accident in childhood had caused him to lose a lot of schooling. 'So I used to go down to the quay at Polruan, where a lot of the old sailing ship men were, and I used to listen to them talking.' Those proud old seadogs had opinions of their own about the new-fangled vessels which were ousting the traditional sailing ships, and those who served aboard them:

'I used to hear them say, "Oh yeah, he's going t'sea, yeah. But he's in a *steamboat* with a thing going around in the back, *pushing*. That isn't sailing, that's just *steering*!", and they went on like that.

'And there'd be some old skippers. They would all be

under the shelter of the linney on the quay, and I'd look at one and say, "Please, sir, can I come in?" I wouldn't be told to come in – he'd point a finger, then his finger would go across his mouth, and point at me again, as if t'say I could, if I kept quiet. So I would sit there, and one of the old skippers would say, "Mr Bosun, get all 'ands aft." And a man who'd been bosun on his ship would stand up, and stamp his foot on the concrete floor three times: bump! bump! bump! One day he done it and he was singing: "*I think I heard our Cap'n say, we'll 'ave some grog t'day.* All 'ands present, sir." Then he'd say those words again: "I think I heard our Cap'n say we'd 'ave some grog today!" There was another one who sang "*Goodbye, fare thee well, I kissed my Kitty on the pier, Goodbye, fare thee well, soon we'll be in Liverpool town ...*" It was really lovely to hear them.

'Well, I'd be in the boats a lot. I knew the men that wouldn't tell me off and I used to go in their boats. Wash them down, bail them out, paddle them and put people aboard, and earn a copper or two. One old man, he was called Tamlyn, Cap'n Bill Tamlyn. Used to be cap'n of a brig, but his eldest son fell over the cliff at Polruan and the old chap went to pieces after that. He stayed home from the sea and was what they called a hobbler. There was no pilots, so he used to bring the ships in and out, and shift them and work on them. His boat was called *Queenie* and I used to like her because she was a nice boat to row and to scull.

'I suppose when I was eight years old I could scull a boat anywhere. I was standing on the thwart one day, sculling, and a chap coming ashore from a ship called out, "I want you! Come here!" So I went in and he said, "If you stand on that thwart again and scull, I'll put that rope around you and you won't sit down for a week!" He said, "You stand down there and scull. If you stand up there and go overboard, you'll drown afore anybody can get down for 'e." And I never stood on the thwart again.

'Another old chap, called Climo, he was an old sailing

Net mending at Polruan around 1910. (Cornish Studies Library)

ship skipper, but he stayed home from sea and went fishing. So he used to take me out with him, hauling lobster pots, and hauling nets. I think by the time I was ten years old, I could cut out and mend a net. They used to show me, and I used to watch them. And it used to be good.

'The ferry that ran from Polruan to Fowey was a motor boat that took twelve passengers, and the man who ran her was Cap'n Jim Burns. The fare was a penny return. I used to go on this here ferry and collect the fares. Then one day he let me drive the engine, and that's how I became interested in engines. When the ferry was sold and I wasn't wanted no longer, another man with a fishing boat, he said, "You come and help me in my boat." So I went fishing with him. Then when I was 14 years old, I said to my mother and father, who had a little bootshop, I'd love to go to sea. They said I couldn't, but I did!

'I had two years in a wooden ship, a wooden ship with seams. When she went in for "ammer and caulkin", I went to work for a blacksmith and engineer called Charles Toms. Another job I done was, I drove a motor launch for the Rockside Hotel. Took people out for pleasure trips. Then in the winter I went to Mevagissey, and went in a herring drifter. That was just a seasonal sort of job, from about the end of October until the end of February. And when they finished the herring driving, the skipper, Mr Barbary, said to me, "Now then, old man, we've finished the herring, now we'm going lining, so you'd better stay with us." So I stayed in her then, and went long lining. Then the fishing got very bad. So I come back home, and drove the motor launch for the Rockside Hotel again.'

It was quite a breakthrough for Claudie when he was able to acquire his own boat, and be his own master.

'She was called the *Rosemary*. I got some financial help from a gentleman to get her. *Rosemary* was a fishing boat. She had two bunks in the cabin and she also had a little kitchen stove – coal burning. I used to take people out on fishing and pleasure trips in her. The harbour master, Cap'n Collins, he used to say to me, "Are you booked up?" "No, sir." "All right, come and see me at my office in an hour's time." And then he'd say, "Now look, I've got this letter from … and he's coming to the Rockside Hotel, and he wants a nice boat recommended …".'

Claudie then went on to mention a string of film stars, titled people and notable personalities of the day, taking it all in his stride and creating a lasting bond with many of them.
One of Claudie's favourites was the Earl of Llanfachraeth.

'I used to take him and his family out. And he used to like to eat boiled mackerel. Then one day he said about cooking and eating them aboard. So I cleaned a couple of mackerel, lit the stove, boiled a saucepan of water, and put them in. And he really enjoyed them, so after that he'd always have a couple of boiled mackerel. He'd be sitting down, eating away and talking away at the same time, and really enjoying hisself. Used t'be nice having people like that!'

This period of independence, operating his own boat, was obviously a happy and fulfilling one for Claudie. It came to an end with the Second World War, when the *Rosemary* was requisitioned by the Navy – which is another story! (See Chapter 10.)

Chapter 3

The Proud Seafaring Traditions of Cadgwith

The sturdy seafaring community of the remote settlement of Cadgwith, whimsically described as 'a romantic fishing village' in a guidebook of 1865, has long enjoyed a well earned reputation for first class seamanship, with a strong tradition of sons following fathers, not only into fishing, but into every branch of maritime service. The Cove supplied young men for the Royal Navy, the Merchant Service and the Coastguard. They were employed as pilots and distinguished themselves in the Cadgwith and Lizard lifeboats. They were also skilled boatbuilders.

In 1885, the *West Briton* had described the scene: 'Cadgwith is a tiny fishing village some distance from the Lizard. There is a bench against the white walls of the cottages right in the centre of the village, from which the whole of the bay can be seen, and from which the boat is watched that is perpetually on the look out for signs of pilchards. On this bench the fishermen sit in patience and wait for the harvest, they scarcely turn their eyes from the sea.'

Mellowed fishermen were still occupying the bench in the time-honoured way when I passed through in 1991, including the then 85-year-old William Arthur and 89-year-old Bert Wylie. They told me that the bench, known to one and all as 'the Stick', was originally an old log washed up from the sea, and placed there for the fishermen to sit on. 'Bin here since the year dot, I should imagine,' mused Bert. ''Twas full of barnacle holes, an' lasted till it wore out or got washed away. An' that was here some years, that old piece of wood. We've had one or two since then.'

'When the fishermen came in from the sea, they'd sit on the Stick, all the fishermen of the Cove,' said William, remembering his childhood days. 'About 20 men as a rule.'

'We weren't allowed to sit on the Stick,' added Bert. 'You weren't allowed to listen to men's conversations. It was a privilege to sit here.'

'As youngsters we used to try and listen to what the men were talking about,' continued William. 'Well, it wasn't long before someone would say, "What do you want?" "Oh, nothing." "Well, get out of it!" An' you'd probably get a clip round the ear!'

These Old Timers, who had themselves led tough lives, remained in awe of those who went before them, and had earned their places on this elite seat after leaving school and proving their worth in the fishing boats.

'You used to be able to sit on this seat and see the *Queen Mary, Queen Elizabeth, Ile de France,* the *America, Rotterdam, Amsterdam, Europas* and *Mauritania* – all pass across the horizon,' mused William when I returned on another cold winter's morning, and the sight of those elegant liners had obviously captured his youthful imagination. We went on to talk about Cadgwith's worldwide seafaring traditions as we adjourned to his home in a pleasing leafy situation above the Cove, with many of the local men spending years in the Navy.

He told me:

'Here in Cadgwith it was all fishing, it was a busy fishing community. There were big families. In the days when seineing was on, about 70 or 80 men with shares in three concerns, fished out of here, coming from as far away as Porthleven. The old schoolroom at the head of the Cove was a seine loft, and there were brick fish tanks, where oil was pressed and sold to Italy, along with the pilchards. The shellfish were in the summer season, and the pilchards in the fall, starting about August. It was the big shoals of pilchards which died out, and seines were no longer used. The seine nets were sold for covering fruit trees. It was drift nets after that, from Porthleven and Mevagissey. So from here it was the shellfish, from about 1900. Now, mostly crab and a few lobsters. When we were boys you'd get a penny for a crab. It was one shilling and sixpence for a lobster, whatever size it was.

'I started fishing as soon as I left school, in 1920. But my brother and I had always been out in the boats with Father, and messing around with them. Used to start going to sea at 14. You'd get up at 3 o'clock in the morning to go to sea. In those days you did what you were told. We'd catch all our own bait; got the crab pots from St Keverne. Fishermen used to wear leather seaboots above the knee, all-weather seaboots, and as they got old they'd become as stiff as a piece of wood.

'This Cove used to maintain everything, one time. If you wanted anything, you made it. One old lady used to use about eight needles knitting fishermen's jerseys. Women used to mend all the nets. Those big pilchard seines that they used had to be mended, and the women did it all. Women used to work very hard in those days – salting pilchards for the winter, salting pollack; salted and dried

Willy Arthur and Bert Wylie aboard the boat Silver Spray *in 1946.
(John Moor).*

out by the sun. Old cottages used to have wooden beams up to the ceilings, and wooden racks for salted and dried fish to be kept for the winter. Salt butter, pickled eggs put in earthenware jars – they'd keep all the winter.'

The wind was in the east when I returned to visit Bert Wylie in his home at the head of the Cove one cold December morning, and nobody was sitting on the Stick. He greeted me warmly as I entered his delightful old cottage, where the walls were adorned with an array of pictures depicting bewhiskered Old Salts, early lifeboats, sailing vessels and steamships relevant to the life of the Wylie family. He stoked up the fire, which crackled merrily in the open grate, and settled down to recall the colourful happenings of this close-knit community.

Bert, who was related to most of the inhabitants of the Cove, explained that his paternal grandfather had come from Scotland to Penzance in the Coastguard service before being drafted to

Cadgwith, and his father had arrived here as a boy. Both of them had fished out of Cadgwith, crewed the lifeboat and served in the Royal Navy. His father had also spent some time in the Merchant service, as he had done.

This part of the coast has collected a catalogue of shipping casualties over the centuries and I asked Bert to highlight the dangers. 'The main hazard is fog,' he said. 'It's all right if you know the rocks; if you can see them. If they don't get clear they've soon had it down there. Because they're all crag rocks, every one of them. The Staggs run out for a mile down there, see? A mile from the shore outwards. And the other one is the Men Hyr Rock. The only time they're out of the water is about from half tide, low, to low water. When the RNLI put a lifeboat to Polpeor it was manned mostly by Cadgwith men. There weren't many fishermen down to the Lizard, as such, in those days. But they were close to the water because they lived by the water.'

Bert's family experienced great hardship during the First World War, when his father was away at sea. 'We had rough times when we never had much grub. In the '14 war the only grub we had come from the sea, washed up. And we sold it to buy commodities. We had barrels of fat. We had oil. We had bags of flour, beeswax and rubber that come in here.'

Bert had worked as a spare hand in the crabbing boats while he was still at school.

> 'Then I went to sea as crew in one of the boats with a man called Bolitho, and went with him during the four years of the war. When his brother George came home, I stepped out of there for 'e to go in his own boat, and then I went with the Coxswain of the lifeboat, Rutter. I was with 'e till the old man sold his boat.
>
> 'Then I went in the Merchant Service. The old man said, "You haven't got any guts" if you wouldn't go. Went to Australia in emigrant ships.' After many happy and fulfilling worldwide adventures, he was pleased to return to Cadgwith to resume his fishing activities in his own boat

and take his place in the lifeboat crew. He married a girl from another lifeboat family. 'I knew my wife for years. We went together for eleven years before we married, 'cos there was nowhere to live. All the houses were full up with fishermen. Each house had its own boat, you see.'

We looked out at the boats drawn up on the beach just outside his cottage window. 'Used to be quite a busy cove. They used to land the coal in here. I've seen two ships at a time in here. Used to carry 100 ton apiece. Come in. Beached. Pulled in tight to high water. And the coal was carried up to a coalyard in carts by an old gent called Captain Joe Nicholls. They were farmers, but they were more or less gentleman farmers in those days. You know, bit better than what we were. The farmers used to have a lot of say here then.'

'Were they allowed to sit on the Stick?' I asked.

'Oh yes, yes. They were part of the fishing industry those days.'

'What were the conversations about when you earned your place on the Stick?'

'Pilchards, chiefly, and fishing. And such things as farmers. We talked about everything. No women would pass the Stick on Sunday evenings – 'cos it would be full of fishermen.'

'There was always fishing people in Cadgwith,' he reflected. Nobody never came here from inland, or anything like that. It was a self-contained community. It was coastal people, and they lived it.' He summed up by saying: 'Life here's been lovely. We've worked hard, and we've fared hard!'

Chapter 4

Coverack – A Close-Knit Fishing Community

Dear Lord, we beseech Thee to watch over our fishermen
out at sea, and bring them safely home.
(a prayer from the shore at times of impending storm)

All around the coast of Cornwall fishing families traditionally occupied compact dwellings close to the shore, where they could keep an eye on the sea and the harbour, in a culture where sons were proud to follow fathers and grandfathers as fishermen and lifeboatmen, ever ready to harness their skills for others.

Things had not changed very much when I visited Mike Eustace at his home in Coverack in December 1991. 'I was born and bred here,' said Mike, 'and my parents, my grandparents, uncles, aunties, cousins and everybody. So we've all had a lifetime of being in Coverack. I've been all over the place, but I've never seen anything better than Coverack.'

I remarked on his delightful cottage looking out across the bay, called Pedn Myin. 'I named it after the rock you see out there,' he said, indicating an area to the west of Lowland Point. 'Well, it started off really as a cows' house years ago. My mother and father had a little property here, which consisted of a garage once owned by an old gentleman. He used to own a big house up the road, and it was a garage for his Rolls-Royce. Mother and Father converted the garage and the outbuildings, which were cowsheds. I converted this one into a little bungalow.'

The waves rolled in relentlessly, and the tamarisks were swaying in the breeze as we stood at the window on that brisk December morning. 'The wind is east-south-east at the moment,' said Mike. 'It's no good for the fishing now; it's impossible to work in the bay in this weather. The boats are all in, and most of them are pulled up as you can see over there on the harbour. I don't miss a thing, actually, concerning the harbour. I can keep my eye on everything from here. There's several boats working from here still. They're all young men and they seem to be getting on all right. In fact I've got a nephew who works from here as well. Yes, they're mostly from traditional fishing and lifeboat families.'

Keeping watch from the shore in the time-honoured way has paid off on a number of occasions, particularly after the closure of the lifeboat station, with appropriate action being taken with inshore emergencies or overdue fishing boats based in the harbour.

It was a tremendous blow to local pride when their lifeboat, which had saved so many lives, was finally withdrawn in 1978. 'There's the son of the Coxswain of the lifeboat, he's still fishing here,' said Mike. 'His name is Carey, and his father was a fisherman called Reginald Carey. In fact, he was the Coxswain who won the Bronze Medal when I was on the boat.'

Part-time fisherman 'Lew' Lewis, who also runs the local gift shop, returns to Coverack harbour and winches his catch onto the quay.
(Dr Derek Hunter)

Mike went on to give a very understated account of the heroic service to the MV *Citrine* of Glasgow in 1956, during which their lifeboat was damaged as she slid over the casualty in a daring manoeuvre which enabled them to save the crew.

'When we came ashore our wives were there to meet us, and when the Coxswain's wife Freda saw the battered bow she called out, "Reggie, what *have* you done? Will you get in trouble by doing that?" We all had a good laugh about that!

'As you know, everybody in my family has been connected with the sea, one way and another   fishermen, lifeboatmen, and my grandfather was a submariner in the First World War. The sea has been in our blood, I suppose. I was in the Royal Marines before becoming the lifeboat mechanic, and I was also an auxiliary coastguard for a short time. I'm still fishing now. There was a Eustace in the first lifeboat that came here [in 1901], Alfred Eustace. He was a fisherman. She was a pulling and sailing boat with six-a-side oars, called the *Constance Melanie*. Then my father went in the boat as a young man, my uncle went in the boat, and I had two cousins in that boat.'

Every inch of this beautiful coastline has a story to tell, particularly the notorious Manacle Rocks to the north-east of Lowland Point, which have claimed countless victims of shipwreck over the centuries. 'That's why they named them the Manacles many years ago. They had such a tight hold that anything that got in there, never got out. I've heard the old fishermen and sailors say that there was so many minerals in the rocks that it made the ships' compasses go "off". The instruments weren't so good as they are now, so ships took the wrong course without knowing it. We've got the Manacles, then there's Lowland Point, Black Head, the Lizard ...'

The sudden descent of mist remains another hazard for fishermen and others less familiar with these waters. 'When you're out at sea, you sometimes see it coming in around the end of the Points, round Chynhalls Point or over Lowland Point. You just see the Points gradually disappear – and then you head for home. By the time you get in you can't see a thing. Thick fog distorts perception. Even experienced fishermen out in their boats might see a rock they pass every day, but wouldn't recognise it. If you see a seagull in the fog, it looks like a swan. You wouldn't believe it, but it's true.'

Mike went on to cite the remarkable skill and knowledge of fishermen and lifeboatmen Cedric Staples and Archie Rowe.

'After we'd gone out looking for a boat missing from the Helford one evening, we headed back, but couldn't see a thing. So we steered by compass. Then Cedric Staples, the Acting Coxswain, who'd been at the helm for some hours, handed over to someone else while he had a smoke. The crewman who took over altered the course very slightly, which landed us in amongst the rocks. After a great deal of consideration, Cedric said, "I think I know where we are. I think we're right in Pedn Myin." So we edged out very, very quietly, and found the channel. Then he took up another course, brought us right across the bay, and we finished up on the lifeboat slip!

'Cedric went fishing with Archie Rowe, who became the Coxswain of the lifeboat. Archie lodged with him and his parents. He was a real character, he was. A massive man with a 24-inch neck. Strong as an ox! Archie had a reputation for his remarkable seamanship, and one time I was there the Inspector said, "If I blindfolded you, Archie, and took you out, could you find your way in?" So Archie said, "Yes." And he was took out there, and we went around the bay, circled around and did all kinds of things, while he just sat in the stern, blindfolded.

'Then the Inspector said, "Now, Archie, do you think you could take her back to the slipway?" "Yeah," says Archie. And he got up on the wheel, and he took her right back into the lifeboat slip. "How did you do it?" exclaimed the Inspector. "Well, I aren't a clot," said Archie. "The wind was sou'westerly when we went out, and was sou'westerly when we came back. So I kept it on one quarter going out, and one quarter coming back!"'

Another example of outstanding seamanship occurred in November 1951, when Archie and his crew saved 17 people from the SS *Mina Cantiquin* of Gijon, which had struck Black Head one dark and stormy night, and was being driven towards Chynhalls Point.

'He got awards not only for rescuing the crew, but also for attempting to rescue the dog. After they'd taken off the survivors, the ship drifted right across the bay. The seas were lifting the side and going right over the top; she was under a mountain of sea most of the time. But because there was a dog in the wheelhouse, Archie returned and made two attempts to get into the ship and get it out. I don't know of another man who would have done that ... and the crew as well.'

Mike chuckled as he recalled one of Archie's exploits during the Second World War.

'There was a barrage balloon which broke adrift from Falmouth. And this barrage balloon was blown overland in the wind and came down across Coverack Bay, trailing a wire hawser with it. Archie said, "I'm going to get that". So he went out in his little boat called the *Bessie*, and made this wire hawser fast to the bow. Then he came back in, with the bow being lifted out of the water. Every time there was a puff of wind, the bow went straight up in the air!

'Well, anyway, we got him into the slipway with this hawser still attached. So he decided that the best thing he could do was to go up and get some weights to put in the *Bessie* to keep her down while he rang up Falmouth to get somebody to take the barrage balloon away. And I shall always remember it – he went down the slip carrying these half-hundredweights, two in each hand, carrying them as if they were just little stones, you know. He anchored this barrage balloon and they came around with an ML as they used to call it in those days – motor launch – from Falmouth, and picked it up and took it back again. Oh, he was a character!'

Chapter 5

Gorran Haven Retrospective

During the 19th century there were long-standing disputes between the fishermen of Gorran Haven and those of Mevagissey, on account of the entanglement of fishing nets. Later on, when the Gorran men had gone over to crabbing, the Mevagissey men would accuse their rivals of mooring their pots to obstruct drift fishing, and severing and sinking their nets. A legacy of all this lingered on into the 20th century, when marriages between Mevagissey lads and Gorran girls led to mutterings in some quarters. Henry Johns, who became Harbour Master here in the 1980s, remarked somewhat wryly, 'They wouldn't have me back now!' He moved to Gorran Haven when he married in the 1930s. 'I worked from Mevagissey still, and went to and fro on a push-bike. Did crabbing and netting, lining, and all different kinds of fishing.

'See, this place here, Gorran Haven, 'twas once at the forefront of the pilchard industry. 'Twas more important than Mevagissey; a bigger place than Mevagissey was then.

That's going back a long time. Them days they used to cure the pilchards and send them to the Continent, by sea from here to Fowey in small barges. Merchants took them aboard bigger craft, barquentines and things like that, to go to south-west France and Italy.'

As we stood inside the fascinating old building at the head of the cove, then used to store the fishermen's equipment, Henry explained:

'This was built for the pilchards. Pilchard cellars, to salt, press and store them. There can't be many of these left in Cornwall, if any, so 'tis appropriate that there's one left here. They used to lay the pilchards in barrels, salt them – layer of fish – layer of salt – layer of fish, and bring them up to the top of the barrel. Then they would press them with round stones with holes in them. See all these holes in the wall, right round? Well, that's where they used to stick the planks in, to provide leverage: stick the end in that hole, and hang the stone outside for weight. And the oil did run down here, along by the wall in the wood floor gutters, and went into barrels. Later on they had big tanks for the oil to go into. They used to burn the oil in lamps, for greasing the slipways for launching boats, all sorts of things.

Sitting comfortably by the fireside in his delightful home on the hill high above the haven, with a canary chirping merrily in the background, Lewis Billing cast his mind back to the days when the Haven was the scene of purposeful workaday maritime activity, and boats filled the harbour.

'There was *Energy*, the *Linnet*, the *Cuckoo*, the *Queen* and many more, all made here by the Pills, who had a boatyard down where the café is now. They built a lot of boats for Mevagissey – fishing luggers, 40 to 50 ft.

Crab and lobster pots were made by local fishermen, as here at Port Isaac in 1943. (George Ellis Collection, Cornish Studies Library)

'The old fish cellars were known as the stores, and we used to put boats in there sometimes. 'E was dry, so you could paint them up, like. Well, those days 'twas nearly all tar, not much paint. Nearly all the boats were black, and they had a yellow stripe around what we call the moulding. These boats were about 18 ft, because we had to pull them up and down. We used to have these 'ere rollers – put them on the rollers and pull them up.

'They were all open boats and nearly all carvel built – oak, larch, or something like that – and tarred. A lot of them used to be sailing boats before the motors come in. They had a foresail and a mains'l, with a sprit and a mizzen. They used to make a lot of the sails at Mevagissey. There was a lot of maintenance. They had to keep scrubbing the bottom off, for the weed and all that sort of thing.

'In the 1800s they had an ochre mine over there on the cliff above Perhaven Beach. There was a platform built on the rock for loading vessels, and they had a trolley with wire ropes going up and down the cliff. The full one would pull the empty one up and they had a big bell over there, a buoy. Made a lot of noise. Shoals of mullet used to come around near the shore, they days in the fall of the year. Always used to come, shoal after shoal, and they'd keep look-out and pull them in on the beach. But this stopped happening, and the fishermen reckoned the noise scared them away. They went over there and there was murder about it! The mining people, they had a boat there, and they capsized that boat. And they had to go to St Austell in the court, and they got fined!

'Done all sorts of fishing. We used to catch grey mullet and bass and pollack and mackerel. Not much pilchards nor herring fishing, 'twas crabs and lobsters, mainly. We used to make crab pots, called them "inkwell pots" [named after the unspillable-style inkwells set in the traditional oak desks in schoolrooms]. Used to use withies – there was all allotments and withy gardens up above the old lime kiln, round the back where there's houses now. And they used to grow them up at C'r'ayes [Caerhayes] Castle. If we didn't have enough, we'd buy them down there for about a shilling or eighteen pence a bundle. I'm still making me own pots. I make about a dozen and a half at a time – used to make 18 to 20 dozen. We never bring in the withy pots. When the first lot was gone, you had to fall back on the second lot of them. One summer in June we lost 120 pots, knocked up in a gale of wind.

'Always used to get out in the morning, regular four o'clock. Generally used to get in, perhaps, twelve or two o'clock. All depends if you get any trouble, like, get the nets and pots caught in the rocks and struggle to get them up. You go out and haul the pots and you take what's in, bait them and put them down, and then you go to the next lot and do the same. Then you go out the next morning and do the very same thing!

'I had a boat built for me specially, down at Porthleven. She was 18 ft 6 inches; we wouldn't have no bigger boats because of dragging them up. For the latter years I've kept her in Mevagissey, only that was a nuisance, going fore and back, fore and back all the time. I had to buy a little car, but first, before I had the car, me and 'Enry [Johns] used to push-bike there.

'I went fishing all the time with my father till I went away in the war. Then after the war he retired and I went with my youngest brother. He bought a boat called the *Coral Reef* from Uncle and it could be worked by two people. We had a winch for pulling the pots up, and that made the pulling a lot easier. It's hard work, you know, dragging them up.

'Fishing – it all depends on the weather. We used to wear leather boots up to here [thigh length] with nails in the bottom, and to keep the water out, tar them all over 'cos they were inclined to be porous and let in water. And big jumpers, generally home-made. Wore just an ordinary cap, and had a sou'wester for rain. And for oilskins, you used to put boiling linseed oil on them, cover them all over and leave them out to dry. They used to be yellow, like. But you can't keep them waterproof, not really. They used to crack, especially where your arms bend. 'Twas pretty uncomfortable. Specially with water going down your neck!

'Superstitions? Rabbits? Whistling? I don't take much notice of that – but I don't like starting on a Friday. They always reckoned it was unlucky, starting fishing on a Friday. A lot of us still believe it, you know. Any day but Friday! Another thing I don't like – somebody wishing you good luck when you go out. Sometimes took visitors out fishing, and I don't think I've been out in the boat only once with anybody with an umbrella. I don't think that's bad luck or anything. But you're in a little ship. And nobody should go out with an umbrella.'

Chapter 6

Fishy 'Gissey

Back along, life in Mevagissey revolved around the harbour, where the quayside was the domain of a proud breed of fishermen. Time was when the harbour was filled to overflowing with fishing boats; time was when the quaysides echoed to the purposeful sound of maritime activity; time was when the whole place reeked of fish, and excited seagulls wheeled and screamed and swooped, and fishermen were busy in their

The seagulls created quite a spectacle in Mevagissey, after the lorries deposited the entrails of the gutted fish over the end of the pier. (Tom and Pat Endacott)

boats or occupying the harbourside benches, musing about the price of fish, boats and happenings, the weather and how things used to be.

Fishermen's sons were absorbed into this way of life on the quayside from a very early age, and enjoyed the camaraderie and the humour, while their daughters were obliged to play a more domestic role. In the early 20th century few of their womenfolk had first-hand experience of activities on the waterfront. Janie Thomas was an exception and recalled her happy association with the fishing scene, explaining that this unusual state of affairs had come about because of her mother's ill health: 'My father, Harry Fulfit, brought me up and therefore I took notice of everything he did. I was on the harbour a lot with him, and would go out in the boat. He had a boat of his own, called after me – *Little Janie* – and I went fishing with him in the afternoons, when my mother could spare me.'

Henry Johns, who was contemporary with Janie, came from a family of fishermen and lifeboatmen, with a strong tradition of service as pilots. 'I was born in 1905,' he told me when I met him in the 1980s. 'My father was a fisherman all his life. He had a boat with his two brothers, a lugger built down Porthleven, called the *Lizzie*. She was 40 ft, the biggest here in them days. That was turn of the century, there weren't motors then. She was built pitch pine on oak, for £198 – two masts and a mizzen sail, and a mainsail on the foremast, and a smaller one to put up when 'twas windy.

'Sails were made in Mevagissey by a man called Lelean. They was white when you had them, and then they had to tan them with the cutch water. We called it "barking" them and 'twas done in barkhouses. We had two or three barkhouses; there was one down on the pier, and one over to the Valley road, as 'tis now, and a man called Furse had three. They had a big furnace with a fire in under, and a great dish we used to call a copper, full of water. The cutch was put in and boiled out – "Burma cutch". And then they

Sails and rope were prepared locally: rope-tarring at Sennen Cove in 1934.
(Cornish Studies Library)

put the sails in. The nets were done the same way. That was in my day, before that the oak trees were barked for curing the nets and that.

'Some of our relations were pilots as well as fishermen, Trinity pilots – my father's grandfather and brothers were pilots for Fowey and Mevagissey and all around here. They used to do that with the fishing. If they were out fishing and there was a vessel coming up and they hoisted their country's flag on her foremast, and if the flag had a white band around the edge of it, that denoted they were wanting a pilot. If they had what we called the "Jack" up – the Union Jack – they'd know it was a Britisher. By night the vessel would put a paraffin flare up.

'They had to have a licence for to be a pilot. They had pilot cutters in Mevagissey and they would go out from here. They used to carry their pilots' clothes with them in a little bag, portmanteau like, and go in the cabin or cuddy and put the gear on, and their hat. And then the cutter would go alongside the vessel, check their licence with them, and put Uncle Robert or one of them aboard, and he would take her in.

'There were other pilots in Mevagissey as well as my family, the Johnses. There was the Clokes, and there was a bit of rivalry between them, you know, getting to the vessels. Pilots were on watch from the sea, the cliffs and all around. Word would come along, such and such a vessel is due somewhere, and they'd be on the watch. See, these other pilots would be watching too, and they used to sneak away sometimes in the gig, no lights up or nothing. Sneak away into the night to get out alongside the vessel to secure the trade.

'The Trinity pilots, they would go aboard the vessel and they paid them so much per foot, so if it was a long vessel they paid more money. On a big vessel it depended on what water they drawed, and that was displayed on the side. It wasn't a lot of money in those days, but then some of them used to get money out of it. Vessels would take a pilot for safety reasons. They could bring them in themselves, but if they did any damage they'd be sued. If they took a pilot they were safe, see? So most reasonable men would take advantage of a pilot.

'In my childhood there were no holidays nor nothing like that. Them days I used to be down around the pier, and the beaches and played in the boats all the time. Mostly in the boats getting into trouble. We used to go aboard Father's boat. These luggers, they'd go out at night time long lining, and netting and things like that. And of course they had a little coal stove aboard, and they used to make their tea. They had condensed milk, and they used to punch a hole in one side of the tin, and another on the other side so they could pour the milk out. We'd get up in the cupboards and drink the milk. Then there was murder next day, when they'd gone out and there wasn't any milk there. We used to get in trouble that way!

'Them days only one or two boats went out on a Sunday. All the rest observed the Sabbath. Went to chapel, a lot of them, but a lot of them didn't. My mother and father never went to chapel, but they still observed the Sabbath.

'I left school when I was 14 – that was 1919, I suppose – and I went fishing. 'Twas sails, you know, there was only one or two that had motors. And then the motors started coming in more, till we done away with the sails altogether. But you used to carry them still, in case you wanted them.

'The mizzen was the main sail then, for to more or less steer the boat when you was getting in the fishing gear, because you were going slowly getting the lines or nets in. The sail would be up, and then you could be working instead of standing up or steering of her. 'Twas long lining in the spring – ray, ling, turbot, pollack, all that sort of fish. The pilchards died out just before the First World War. And then they came back again, so we went into having nets for pilchards then. My latter years, we used to do quite a bit of pilchard driving. We'd go seven or eight mile off, sometimes a bit further. Then, as the summer come on, come August month, the pilchards used to come in here in the bays. We used to shoot along the bays, along down Gerrans Bay, Hemmick, places like that.

'Used to eat a lot of pilchards, them days. See, you had the fish for nothing and 'twas a good feed then for very little money. If there was no fishing we had them marinaded. Mother used to do a big bowlful; keep you going for a week. Gut the pilchards, take all the gut out and then give them so much salt – get the salt through them. And then they had spices, cloves and all, and some kind of olives. Mother used to do them with half vinegar and half water, baked in the oven. She'd leave them in the

Mevagissey harbour in the 1950s, when the old Lifeboat House was being used as a café. (Mevagissey Museum)

dish and you'd take them out as you wanted them, have them cold. Keep you going for a week! I had a sister and three brothers, and we used to have them for tea. I've done a few, latter years. Oh, they'd be lovely!

'Mevagissey Feast, that was a big week, the end of June. All the boats were racing – all the luggers sailing. There wasn't much money in the prizes. If they went out, three or four hands or more – nine or ten in one of the luggers – and got First Prize, that would be seven shillings and sixpence. That was very little money. 'Twas all done for the fun, you know.

'There was a lot of characters around them days. Back years ago there used to be an old man called 'Enry 'Ocking, a big chap, used to go shooting nets up Bigbury Bay in wintertime. "We went out," he said, "and 'twas bad weather. Weather wasn't very good at all." So he decided, we'll have a cup of tay and we'll haul away early, get away out of it. So he told this old man, Sam Longley, the oldest of the crew, to go and make the tay. So Sam goes in fer making the tay. And after a bit they come in and ask, "Where's the tay?"

"I've made the tay," he said, "but I can't find my pipe nowhere." He used to smoke a clay pipe with the end broke off, and to keep the old stump in his waistcoat he wore over his jersey. "I can't understand where my pipe is to," he said, feeling around and putting his finger in his waistcoat pockets. Then 'Enry jumped to it. "Give us the spoon up there," he said. And he fished around in the pot and out comes this pipe. "Here you are, Sam," he said, "here's your pipe!" And Sam said, "Well, I'm blessed." Sam had drinked his tay and never knowed!'

Chapter 7

The Falmouth Scene

One of the most familiar faces to be seen around Falmouth's waterways, kindly, suntanned and ever ready to break into a smile, belonged to fisherman George Vinnicombe, who came from a seafaring family of Devon stock.

When his grandfather and father left Devon for Mylor, attracted by the oyster dredging, they had a fishing smack with the beguiling name *The Silent*. 'They used to go oyster dredging in winter, and trawling in summer around the Dodman and the Lizard in a quay punt,' said George, who went on to explain that oyster dredgers, now known as working boats, evolved from the Falmouth quay punts, which were deep-keel boats designed for putting to sea and speediness in meeting the incoming merchant vessels. 'The oyster dredgers have a shallow draught, to allow them to drift over the oyster beds The Falmouth working, dredging boats raced, and they still do. When the working boats are racing, we are great rivals, but we're great friends again when the race is over. My uncles used to race *Florence* and the *Six Brothers* in regattas.

Some of the characters of the Falmouth waterfront at the beginning of the 20th century. (John Miles)

'St Mawes men, St Just men, Fowey men, Porthleven men, all used to come up and go fishing. My grandfather said you used to be able to see the estuary full of working boats. It was quite a big thing. They used to sail over from France to buy our oysters at half a crown a thousand.'

We cast our minds back to less sophisticated days, when life was harder, more colourful and more fun. 'In the old days, when you got tired, you just rolled up in a sail,' recalled George nostalgically.

'You wore tough, leather boots. They all had them in Falmouth. And when the boots wore out, the leather was used for leathering the paddles around the padlock and for lining the boom jaws. Nothing was ever wasted. It was a big thing, and a lot of expense, getting a pair of boots made and specially fitted. We used to have to dub our boots with beeswax to keep them waterproof and to keep the leather supple. Your oilskins were the same, see? You'd get smocks made at the sailmakers, out of ordinary sailcloth, and what you'd do, you'd get it wet and then paint it, or else it would crack. You'd do that two or three times and it came to be waterproof. Nobody don't do that no more, now. Wintertime, when it was very cold, you'd put newspapers inside for insulation. All the old fishermen used newspaper. It was a wonderful way to keep the wind out.

'We all wore tammy shanters, you know, "Johnny Onion" hats. When we were younger these Frenchmen used to come across in little sailing schooners with two or three tons of onions. They had a store ashore. They'd come in the harbour, and cycle all over Cornwall on their push-bikes, heavily laden with strings of onions about five or six feet long, all hanging down, and they'd go from house to house selling them. We'd all look out for Johnny Onions.'

Falmouth's fishing fleet in the early 1900s. (Sheila Bird Collection)

But times change.

> 'My grandfather was the first to have an engine put in his boat, and it paid for itself in fish caught in the first week. But *The Silent* was not so silent after that! Then there was *Boy Willie*. I've still got *Boy Willie*! She is 150 years old, a 31-footer. She was originally built at Porthleven. Father had her brought from Mevagissey, partly sail, with one engine. After a while he had two engines put in her, twin engines, side by side. They were in there from the time I was a boy, and I worked them for 30 years.
>
> 'I was fishing *Boy Willie*, and I acquired *Six Brothers* for oyster dredging, built by 'Foreman' Ferris for old Jimmy Lewarne. She was in a sorry state.'

George, like others of his breed, had a very close relationship with his craft, and still felt very sadly about the loss of his beloved *Six Brothers*.

George Vinnicombe, as a young lad, aboard the family boat, Boy Willie. *(Vinnicombe family)*

'It was a bad south-east gale, and we landed at Mylor, near Greatwood Wood. The boats ran aground a little further upstream. They got *Mildred* off, but *Six Brothers* broke her drift and sailed up on the rocks. From the Dockyard Pier we saw she broke her moorings, ran alongside us and became dashed on the rocks. She listed out, sea broke aboard and burst her side out. It was one of the saddest moments of my life. We salvaged all we could. We won a lot of prizes with her ...

'Percy Dalton, using the keel and some of the fittings, reconstructed a new *Six Brothers*. It was supposed to be a replica, but I've not got the same feelings for her.'

Percy Dalton, who died tragically in the early 1980s, had been a much respected man of the Falmouth scene, and was a close friend of George's. 'He was a wonderful chap, one of the best designers. He had a great flair for it and built boats for all over the world.

'When I started fishing you worked with your eyes, your ears and your head. You watched for all the signs – the colour of the water, the movement of the birds. Now it's all done with instruments. You jump aboard, turn on your Dekker navigator before you leave the moorings. Then you steam to the area where you normally find fish, and turn on your fish finder, an instrument with a black screen. Anything shows up, plankton or fish, it comes up in different colours and you can tell what kind of fish is there. It's all got so sophisticated.' With prescience he added, 'If we don't get regulations put on certain types of fishing in a few years' time, there will be nothing left to fish.'

Yarning at the Chain Locker

In the 1980s, when the quayside was their domain, the colourful characters of the Falmouth waterfront would adjourn to the Chain Locker from Custom House Quay for a drink or two and a yarn.

'Back when there were sailing ships coming in all the time to Falmouth, a lot of the waterside pubs like the Chain Locker here – well, it was the Marine Hotel, really – played an important role in the maritime scene,' explained Jimmy Morrison.

'At the Globe they catered particularly for sea captains, because one of the rooms was always called The Captain's Room, and it was rare that anyone, apart from the shipping fraternity, ever set foot in it. There would be old sea captains having a yarn or doing business with their agents; it was their little place.

'As far back as I can remember, the Chain Locker was kept by Tom Richards. That was in the Twenties. It was a very popular pub in those days with the coal porters. We had the two elevators putting steam coal aboard ships, which was a very arduous and dusty job, and they used to come in here and wash all the dust down after they'd conquered a vessel. The fishermen frequented the waterside pubs in Falmouth and all around the waterways of the Fal, and there were quite a lot of colourful characters. A tough lot. They had to be.'

Jimmy Morrison, seafarer, boatman and oyster fisherman, who had spent a lifetime on the waterfront and had a remarkable knowledge of Falmouth, the river and its characters, was recognised as being Falmouth's link with its proud and colourful past. Sitting outside the Chain Locker nearly 30 years ago, we surveyed the much loved maritime scene and talked about the old days.

Jimmy's family had been part of Falmouth's seafaring history for generations. 'The Morrisons have been in the boating business in the Falmouth area, and particularly Falmouth, for the past 150 years,' he declared proudly. 'Originally they came from the Isle of Lewis in Scotland, where they were kicked out for sheep stealing. They went from the Isle of Lewis to Southern Ireland, from where they came to Falmouth in a sailing ship around 1835, and established themselves in the boating business on the Falmouth Custom House Quay.

'They seem to have prospered with the increase in the world shipping trade. After 1830 the ships became larger and faster as they went into the clipper ship era, from about 1840 to 1890, but it had finished by the time the Suez Canal was built. My family acquired one or two ships for the business. One particularly, the Falmouth quay punt *ICU*, was instrumental in establishing the family as premier boatmen in the area. This boat was built for my grandfather, Walter Morrison Senior, around 1894 by R.S. Burt of Bar Yard, Falmouth. Things flourished for quite a number of years, and with the decline of sailing ships around the early 1920s, they turned over to motorboats.

'Custom House Quay used to be a very interesting little basin in the 1920s, when I was a boy. To come down here of a Sunday morning and look at all the little vessels that was tied up here – the little tops'l schooners like the *Snowflake*, *Earl Cairns*, the *Alert*, *Mary Barrow*, come in here to discharge house coal alongside the wall over there on the North Quay. The *Mary Barrow*, a three-masted and tops'l schooner, was a lovely little vessel. Peter Mortensen, Peter the Viking, was her master. You could spend hours looking at them all.'

As a small boy, Jimmy enjoyed helping out on his father's boats, and he was expected to be capable.

'I remember back in 1928, when I was in my father's barge called the *Swift*, up at Pentewan, and we had a loaded cargo of concrete blocks. He was towing me down in his fishing boat and when we got off Mevagissey we ran out of paraffin. We had to anchor the barge and go into Mevagissey to get a supply of paraffin to carry on around the Dodman. Anyhow, when I got out to the Dodman in the old *Swift*, the wind came round from the south'ard and me father said, "You get the mainsail on her." Then he said, "You can make down to St Anthony now." And he gave me an old mackerel line and carried on and left me, a boy of about ten or eleven years old, to sail the *Swift* back to Falmouth alone! I'll never forget that, for as she was falling in the sea, the water was coming right over the foredeck and washing aft, and I had to jump on top of the companion hatch aft to keep the water from coming over the top of me little short seaboots.'

Jimmy Morrison's dad, Norman, known to one and all as 'Ferret', with the Royal fish, the sturgeon – every sturgeon caught has to be notified to the monarch, who traditionally has the first option. (Sheila Bird Collection)

The evocative cry of the seagulls wheeling overhead and re-echoing around the harbour brought our attention back to the immediate environment and its nostalgic associations.

'We learned to swim from them steps across the Basin, there, in the 1920s, and we progressed from there to longer swims across, from here over to Kiln Quay and back. We could do that in about 25 to 30 minutes each way. It's somewhere about a mile and a quarter over and back and we did that regularly. We all learned to swim very early down here – you either swam or you sank, and that was how it was!

'When my father was about 14, he was helping in the *ICU*, with Sam Coplin in charge. He had orders to go out and bring ashore his elder brother Walter, and Janner Snell, two well-known characters in those days for negotiating ships' business orders for provisions with the captains of sailing ships. Walter and Janner had been taken aboard by tug, and those aboard the *ICU* out in the middle of the harbour were uncertain as to which ship they were on. The twin-funnelled tug *Penguin* went out to the quay punt to let them know which ship it was. In the manoeuvring position to pass on the information, something went wrong with instructions, and the *ICU* was cut in half and sank. Aboard the *ICU* they had anticipated what was about to happen, braced themselves, jumped over the bow pudding fender and were grabbed by the crew who scrambled over the bow of the tug. The tugs used to nudge vessels around with the bow pudding – made of heavy belting – against their side, and this fender protected the boat.

'Eventually the *ICU* was located by local divers and she was raised and repaired. She was completely smashed down one side. She was built of yellow pine planking and was designed to be very fast, but was not so fast after the accident.

'The *ICU* was in close proximity to one of the quay punts, the Fat Boat, or the *Fearnot* as she was really called. She got that name on account of being a boat which collected the fat accumulated from the cooking on sailing ships during protracted voyages. It was manufactured into soap, or boiled up and sold to the poorer people of

Falmouth at a penny a pound. I remember my father telling me about the fate of the poor old Fat Boat. She was pursuing her business down towards the Lizard and trying to meet up with a sailing ship rounding the Lizard under lower tops'ls, because it was blowing hard sou'-west strong. Bill Weatherly and Brian Pascoe were in her. Then she took this nasty sea aboard and she and her crew disappeared with no trace. The *ICU*, only half a mile astern in poor conditions, was unable to render any assistance.'

When Jimmy left school he worked on the ketch-rigged sailing barges which carried roadstone from Porthoustock to points around the Fal and Helford rivers, which were then very busy commercial waterways.

'Barges varied considerably in their size, decking and capacities. Decked vessels, smacks, or 'outside' barges, which plied around Plymouth, Falmouth and the West Country, such as the *Emma*, *J&R* and *Sweet May*, had a capacity of about 75 to 80 tons. 'Inside' or Truro river barges, which carried less than 40 tons, such as the *Swift*, *Sunbeam*, *Marion*, *Maggie*, *Greyhound*, *Little Industry* and *Topsie*, traded around the creeks. In their heyday there were 30 or 40 of these type of barges, with open hold, foredeck and afterdeck, trading up and down the Fal and Truro rivers, Tresillian and up to Ruan Lanihorne. They brought business when everything went by water. The *Mary* and the *Dorothy* had the capacity of about 50 tons, and the *Silex* and the *PHE*, about 60 tons.

'Those carrying 40 tons took in say, 400 bags of barley and the height of the cargo extended about four feet above the deck because the cereals were light in capacity. The cargo sometimes went up so high as six or seven feet and you had to have a short ladder to get up over the top of it to go for'ard. You couldn't see ahead and you were

Jimmy Morrison hauls the dredge aboard in the Carrick Roads. Dredges used in fishing for oysters were netted bags held open with a rigid framework, which were dragged slowly along the river bed. (Jimmy Morrison)

completely blocked aft. You had to nip up on the top and have a look out ahead to see if there was anything in your fairway, perhaps a rowing boat or a sailing boat crossing your bow. Especially when you got in the river Fal during oyster dredging time. For instance, at Turnaware Bar there could be, say, 40 or 50 punts there oyster dredging, and if you come up with a loaded barge you had to nip up every so often to look over the top to see that you weren't running into anybody.

'When the family boat, the *Eclipse,* was beginning to show her age, I turned to dredging for oysters. I went down to Lelant near St Ives where the *Mayflower* was laid up and bought her for £20 from Tom Heeney Freeman. That was in 1937, same year as I got married. She was built by Olivers of Porthleven in 1903 as a rowing sailing crabber; an open boat then. She's a good boat, though she's getting on a bit now.'

We talked about the highly talented boatbuilders of Falmouth and its waterways, who have become legendary. The Falmouth yards produced hundreds of ocean-going and local vessels, while the Ferris, Hitchen and Brabin families are particularly remembered for the oyster-dredging craft which have stood the test of time so well. All were built for speed and seaworthiness.

> 'Oysters are caught when drifting, so the success depends on the manoeuvring capacity to sail back over the ground to start the next drift. Dredging for oysters under sail in the Carrick Roads survives as one of the few things a man can do on his own, with a boat of his own,' commented Jimmy.

The traditional working boats in full sail created a stunning spectacle during the regattas, and their crews liked to demonstrate their skills to appreciative audiences on the shore. Frank Cock recalled the occasion when he was aboard the *Morning Star*, then owned and skippered by Billy Harris. 'As we were turning very tightly on a mark, we jibed too close to the quay and the boom swept a couple of spectators into the water. Fortunately they were not hurt!'

Jimmy Morrison reckoned that the old *Morning Star* was 'something to be reckoned with in smooth water', when she was racing against the quay punts. 'She was constructed in Looe sometime before 1830 and started her life as a seine boat at Portloe. Old Billy Harris's father picked her up when she was lying more or less derelict in a creek off Mylor. He had her lengthened and adapted for dredging.'

The local seafarers, who were masters of their natural domain, tended to feel rather ill-at-ease in the Big City. An Old Timer from Devoran admitted, 'I only once went up to London, I had to go for an exhibition. All the time I couldn't sleep. Dustbins rattling at four o'clock in the morning ...' He looked pained at the recollection. 'Glad to get back and get some rest! I don't like going much other places than Truro and Falmouth. I like the music of the gulls in Falmouth. If I go much further I think I'm going abroad.'

This revelation prompted Tony Warren, the artist and colourful character of the Falmouth waterfront, to tell us about a group of local mariners who went up to London for the weekend.

'One of them got separated from his friends in central London and felt bewildered because he didn't know where he was or where his friends were staying. He asked a policeman if he had seen his friends pass by, and was rather surprised that the policeman didn't know anything about them. "Well, *everyone* do know them in Falmouth," he said. His quest was fruitless, and in the end he took a train home to Falmouth.'

Being in such a close-knit maritime community, where the seafaring fraternity traditionally kept an eye open for their colleagues out on the water, was very reassuring. But it could have its drawbacks. Tony went on to tell us about the occasion when the characters of the waterfront became increasingly concerned about one of their number, whose fishing boat was apparently drifting around in the harbour without any sign of anyone on board.

'They took a boat out to investigate and came upon him I think they call it *in flagrante* ... hard at it ... going great guns in the bottom of the boat. With a young lady who was not his wife!'

Chapter 8

Around the Waterways of the Fal

Those who established small settlements around the waterways of the Fal sought to glean a livelihood from the river, which served as a highway, and from the land.

The Gunns of Coombe Creek and Malpas

For generations the Gunns of Coombe Creek, famous for its plum and apple orchards, went oyster dredging in the season and then used their boats to transport their produce to market.

When I met him some 26 years ago, oysterman Gerald Gunn told me that he fell in with outdoor seasonal work after he left school, as was the custom around these parts. 'We went oyster dredging from October to March, "taking off the bark" [oak bark for the tanning industry] from April to July, and then it was fruit picking time. Practically every house had an orchard, and everybody would sell their own produce in Truro or Falmouth. 'Twas all boat. There were three ways of getting home: if there was a wind you would sail; if there was no wind you would row; but if you had the chance you'd have a tow behind a pleasure steamer. You used your own boat. I've still got her. She's called *Irene* after my wife – nearly everybody used to call their boats after their wives.'

The fishermen of Coombe Creek did not always need to resort to their boats to land a catch, for as Gerald's younger brother Randolph explained, 'We used to put a net right across the mouth of the creek. The net lay on the mud at low water, and lifted at high water to trap the fish. Then we'd wait until the next low water to collect the fish, which would be plaice or mullet. But there are new regulations about the mesh and no one carries on this tradition.' However, he still enjoyed shrimping in the old manner.

Donald Gunn, one of George Gunn's seven children, was brought up at Malpas, where he and his brothers learned to handle boats from a very early age.

'Father was a fisherman on the river, mainly oyster-dredging in winter and fishing in summer, and as a boy I used to go fishing with him. He used 16-ft punts, and went dredging off St Just in Roscland. We'd row down and home, for there were no motors then. It was a pretty tough life, all winds and weathers. In some fishing boats we had four of us, you know, to work the nets. Caught bass, mullet, dabs, pollack, and bream by the million. It was a good river in those days, we got a good living. Father's boat was called *Donald*, after me. I started to work in 1915, when men were going away to war. As soon as I left school, Father bought me a working boat for oyster-dredging, worked by one man, as distinct from fishing boats with four men aboard. She was called the *Primrose*. Soon as I started courting "Mother", I changed the name to *Ray*, in honour of my good lady, short for *Rachael*.

Oyster fishermen hauling in the dredges at the Duchy of Cornwall oyster farm at Port Navas on the Helford in September 1955. The working craft dredging in the Fal and Helford rivers are the only remaining ones in Europe required to operate under sail over the oyster beds.
(George Ellis Collection, Cornish Studies Library)

'I met "Mother" going to chapel. Another fellow and myself used to walk from Malpas to Truro Sunday nights, and we eyed these two girls for some time before we got talking to them. They were two sisters. Got the courage outside the chapel one Sunday evening, and got talking. We were courting for seven years, and we got married in 1929, when I was 22. She was a tailoress, but quit her job the day we were married. She stayed at home, cooked the meals and made all our clothes.

'Before the First World War, every little creek around the river used to have their own regatta; it was mostly rowing, you know. My father George Gunn was reckoned to be the best rower in those days. The very first one after the war at Coombe, I entered that race against my father, and others, and I came in first. After that I won the

Championship of Cornwall for 18 years, missing just one year after an operation. We used to row for the championships at Hayle, and I always used the same boat, the *Diamond*.

'Before the Second World War big shoals of mullet came up the river, and the men used to know when they were likely to arrive. A shoal created ripples on the surface of the water, like a boiling kettle. And they always headed for Tresillian. Then all the fishermen from Malpas, Coombe and places along the river would bring their boats along, and a long, long net, which was stretched right across the river from St Clement to the Tregothnan side. The net would have corks on top and a heavy chain on the bottom, and they would keep the net there for the flow of the tide, till high water. At high water they'd let the chain down, and all the fish were trapped upriver, behind the net. Then at low water the men would walk to Tresillian with a net stretching the width of the channel – one each side, dragging the net and forcing the fish down to the main net. P.H. Tonkin of Truro, who had a shop in King Street, brought a lorry to St Clement to collect the fish. This was called "hacking for mullet". Local folk would go out into the channel and pick up dabs and flounder and other fish that had become trapped in this way. Any fish left over was there for the picking.'

Yarning at the Pandora

It would be difficult to imagine a more picturesque old inn more pleasingly placed than the Pandora on Restronguet Creek. It was originally known as the Passage Inn, for it was situated on the old pilgrim route between Ireland and France, with the landlord being responsible for operating the ferry,

The Pandora has been a favourite haunt of the rivermen for centuries and in the 1980s I met with the Old Timers there for a yarn. One of them told us that in his grandfather's day, when oysters were commanding very low prices, the French used to buy them in bulk. 'Came across March, April time and used to pay the men here, at the Pandora. Used to pay for them in gold sovereigns.' Our present company agreed that the French had always had a penchant for oysters, which few of them shared. As Frank Cock put it, 'Tried one once, but didn't like it!'

Falmouth boatman Jimmy Morrison recalled an engaging member of the Ferris family who has found an enduring place in local maritime folklore.

> 'Jack Ferris, known to one and all as "Tensie", on account of being the tenth of ten brothers, was at one time the landlord of the Pandora. Also he was the owner of the working boat, the *Florence*, and he had several well known relations, including "Foreman" Ferris, who was a famous shipbuilder at Yard on Restronguet Creek. Most of the family were in the seafaring line. They went fishing and oyster dredging.'

Reginald King of Devoran explained that when Tensie took over the Pandora, he also had responsibility for operating the ferry which was summoned from the Feock side by bell.

> 'The bell came off the old ship *Penpole*. In the 1940s our local doctor, Dr Edwards, who spent half his life in Devoran, used to have patients on the other side of the creek. On one occasion when he wanted to get across to see a patient, he tolled the bell, and kept on pulling for some time with no response. The reason for the delay was undoubtedly that Tensie was having a busy time behind the bar.
>
> 'Finally, Tensie came out to him. The doctor, rather a forthright Scotsman, said, "Where the hell have you been to, Tensie? I've been ringing that bell for ages!" Tensie, assuming a suitable look of injured innocence, replied, "'Ave 'ee, doctor? I never heard 'ee." Returning to the pub after attending to his patients, the doctor said to the landlord in a quiet tone of voice, "Will you join me for a

whisky, Tensie?" The ferryman eagerly replied, "I don't mind if I do, Doctor," to which the doctor tartly retorted, "Well, you bloody well heard me that time!"

'Yes,' continued Reginald, 'Tensie was a real character. He used to tell people that the Phoenicians used to come upriver for tin in the old days. He'd get so earnest about it and once got so over enthusiastic about ramming the story home to incredulous listeners that he added, "Yes, I know … because I ferried 'em up the river meself!"

'It sometimes fell to Tensie to act as boatman for the aristocracy, and on one occasion he took some ladies out for a prolonged boating session on the river. Being a thoughtful sort of a man, he became a bit concerned about their comfort, knowing that being upper class didn't necessarily mean that they had a limitless bladder capacity. In an effort to introduce the subject in a polite and tactful way, he began "Er … we've been out in the boat for a long time, and some of you ladies might want … er, be getting a bit uncomfortable … so if you'd like to … er, relieve yourself, like … um," he paused, waiting for inspiration to strike. Having got so far, he couldn't stop now, so to cover his confusion he grabbed a bucket, and thrusting it towards them, blurted out, "You can piss in this 'ere bucket!"'

At that point we were joined by Aubrey Ferris of Devoran, whose great-grandfather was the much revered 'Foreman' Ferris. Casting his mind back to happy childhood days, Aubrey recalled an early watery experience.

'We used to go out in the oyster boat *Harriet* with Grandfather. The three of us, plus Mother and Father, went out one time, when the boat was moored up in the little dock during the winter. We went to bail her out, and I fell over the side as I was playing with a model yacht. Father pulled me out by the feet! I was about seven or eight at the time.'

This prompted boatbuilder and former oysterman Terry Heard to recall,

'The old men of years ago used to tell a tale about Harold Ferris when he was two years old. They used to call him "R". When a boat was being launched someone noticed that "R" was missing. "Where's he got to?' someone asked. "He was sitting on the side of the boat a moment ago," said someone else. Further investigation revealed young "R" floundering in the water, and he was dragged aboard in the nick of time. If he could survive that at the tender age of two, he could survive anything! They were *hard* men. Had to be hard in those days. Out dredging, he would say, "Let her git!" Like talking to horses. "Let her git, boy!" Hard as nails.

'Old Jimmy, as had *Six Brothers* before George Vinnicombe, was a little old chap. His fingers were fixed in the rope-gripping position. He used to go around in his captain's cap, with his white beard. Lived in the village of Mylor. Used to get water from the village pump or collect rainwater, and would wash in his garden. The Skipper would place his enamel bowl of cold water on the marble-topped table out in his front garden, strip right down to his flannel vest and lather up all over his face and his little old bald head. But the Skipper, he was never dirty. Clean as a new pin!'

Everybody chuckled, and Terry reiterated, 'There he was out in the front garden all lathered up, and blowing bubbles everywhere ... *bbblll ... bbblll ... bbbbblll ...* soap everywhere! It was quite a surprise to anyone who happened to be passing by and looking over the gate. And he lived to be 98!'

Chapter 9

Danger and Disaster

The treacherous seas around the Cornish coast have claimed countless lives over the centuries, and gained a certain notoriety amongst mariners worldwide. The Atlantic Ocean has aptly been described as the 'great mother of storms', where fluctuations in temperature and air pressure, and changes in wind direction can give rise to rapidly erupting storms and squalls, or the sudden descent of all-enveloping sea mist. Those who fished these waters faced – and still face – potential danger every time they put to sea.

It was customary for the local seafaring fraternity to maintain vigil from the shore, and to carry out spontaneous rescues in their own boats. When the Royal National Lifeboat Institution was established, their lifeboats were manned mostly by fishermen, who performed exceptional feats of bravery in the humanitarian cause of preserving life from shipwreck.

Barry Mundy, fisherman and longstanding member of the Lizard/Mullion Coastguard Auxiliary, talked about the capricious nature of the elements in the region as we stood on the harbourside at Mullion.

'On a day like today, it's idyllic. The sea's calm and you just couldn't imagine that it could ever be rough – "rough" meaning that the sea could come over Mullion Island. You can have reasonably calm weather, and within an hour and a half it can change into a casualty-risk situation.

'There were a lot of shipwrecks around here in the 1800s. The problem was with the easterly wind. If they couldn't round the Lizard and proceed up-channel, they would pull into Mullion Roads, which in an easterly wind was a safe anchorage. But the problem with the easterly, it always ended where the wind veered to the south, and then south-west. While it was back, say, south-east, it would build up a sea. Because with an easterly wind you've got high pressure, and when the high pressure slips away, you've got a low pressure coming in from the Atlantic. So the wind then would go out to the south-west, and the sea would come in. The ships would then be on a lee shore, and they would try and beat out of the bay. And some made it, and some came to grief.'

I asked what signs the local fishermen looked for before they put to sea.

'You must be watching for signs and casting your eyes to the horizon the whole time you are out. You can get the signs in the sea, probably two to three days before the weather comes. If you're looking down at the pierhead, there, you'll see the strength of the sea. It may appear calm on the surface, but as it pulls around the end of the quay, you get a big swirl and an eddy. And that can happen, say, a couple of days before the weather actually comes in. That's one of the early signs. And then, you know, you've got all the other normal signs in the sky that you look for. And it's different every day that you look at it.'

As fishermen, lifeboatmen and coastguards the Mundy family has a long tradition of going to the aid of people in distress along this coast. We talked of the close bond which has always existed amongst seafarers.

'It's when you've got your back to the wall that you can count on everybody,' Barry said, and went on to give a personal example.

'One day in the 1980s, on a really calm day, I was fishing off Gunwalloe, and everything was going as normal. Then a set of things started to go wrong, and in a matter of five or six seconds I was over the side! The boat was still in gear and it went in, and went on the rocks. And I got picked up about 15 minutes later, by a boat about half a mile away. The irony is that I was 41 years of age, and wasn't able to swim until about a month before I fell overboard! The boat came off the rocks a few minutes later, and the boat that picked me up put me back on board. I had a little damage on the boat; very little, really. And another funny thing about this incident – as I was thinking about how to mend the boat and feeling a bit confused, I said to the person that picked me up, "What day is it?" And he said, believe it or not, "It's Friday the 13th June!"

In his *Survey of Cornwall*, published in 1602, the historian Richard Carew observed: 'Padstow first presenteth itselfe a towne and haven of suitable quality, for both (though bad) are the best that the North Coast possesseth...'. As he also noted: 'The harbour is barred with banks of sand.' Since that time the notorious Doom Bar has claimed countless victims of shipwreck, many of them fishermen.

One sunny morning in October 1990, the Old Timers on the quayside were keen to talk of the halcyon days of yore, when Padstow was a busy port enjoying trading links with Ireland and the Baltic, and fine ships were constructed on the quayside. The hardy and intrepid fishermen were engaged in the great

A workaday scene at Padstow harbour c.1930.
(Royal Institution of Cornwall)

Newfoundland trade, sailing in specially equipped vessels, and away from home for months at a time. This prompted Eddie Murt to quote one of his father's pithy sayings: 'Years ago there used to be iron men and wooden ships, and now 'tis the other way around.'

These fishermen had also served on the lifeboat. Fishermen, pilots, coastguards and other seafarers had carried out spontaneous rescues long before the lifeboat station was established at Hawker's Cove in 1827. The lifeboat was at the heart of the community. 'Everybody ran when the rockets went up,' they said, 'Women and all. They all ran over to Cove, to help launch the lifeboat.' Three lifeboats were operating at Padstow at one time, on account of restricted conditions within the estuary, so a new station was established at Trevose Head in 1967, with a slipway launch into Mother Ivey's Bay.

We adjourned to Alfie Orchard's cottage where, as we enjoyed tea and cake by the fireside, he told me about his eventful life, and how the family adapted to changing circumstances. The youngsters were in awe of their elders and were keen to prove themselves when he was a lad.

> 'My older brother William and I went fishing with Father, so life in boats just come naturally to me.
> 'My brother William, who was about four years older than me, and the first in the family to become a lifeboatman, was awarded a Silver Medal in 1944 when the *Princess Mary* lifeboat went to the aid of the steamer *Sjofna* of Oslo, which had gone ashore north of Bude. He was the Second Mechanic, but was put in command on this occasion because of his experience in very difficult conditions. They saved seven lives.' Acting Coxswain William Orchard also received the Maud Smith Award for the Bravest Lifeboat Deed of the Year.

I asked Alfie about his most memorable experience in the lifeboat, and he told me about rescuing the crew of 18 from the Norwegian steamer *Taormina*, which had got into difficulties while attempting to seek refuge in the harbour during a north-westerly storm in February 1928.

> 'When we went alongside this wreck they was throwing their kitbags and all into the lifeboat. But that was against the rules, and the Coxswain threw them overboard. 'Twas to pick up survivors, not luggage. The kitbags could've bunged up the valves at the bottom of the boat and sunk it.' Coxswain Baker was awarded a Bronze Medal and his crew received Thanks on Vellum for this outstanding rescue. This had been the first service of the lifeboat's crew of 13.

Mrs Orchard remarked: 'People say to me, why do you let 'im go out there fishing? But I know he wouldn't do anything to cause a danger. If he wanted to go, that was his wish. Being out on the sea, that's what makes him happy!'

Eddie Murt also talked about his early life on the Padstow waterfront, which was interrupted by two years' National Service when he was 18. 'Funny thing,' he chuckled, 'being a water boy, knowing mostly about the sea and fishing and that, I had to go into the army! After that I went fishing again. I went crabbing for a firm called Harvey's down at Newlyn, and fishing at Lundy.'

Eddie came from a well known fishing family, who also distinguished themselves in the lifeboat. 'My father was the Coxswain, and my uncle, John Tallack Murt, was the Coxswain of the other lifeboat. My brother Johnny was in the lifeboat, and I served as Assistant Mechanic and Mechanic for 42 years.' John Tallack Murt was awarded the Silver Medal for the courageous service to the SS *Kedah*, carried out in 'almost impossible' conditions in August 1946, in which they saved ten lives.

'Years ago,' said Eddie, 'skippers used to forecast the weather by the wind and the look of the sky, and say, "We'll have a gale o' wind tomorrow" or something like that. My Dad, he was a grand old feller. He used to say, the sea was like a woman. And I'd say, "Why's that, Dad?" And he says, "Very unpredictable. Blow from any angle!" My Mum used to laugh. Another thing he used to say: "If you won't be ruled by the rudder, you'll be ruled by the rock."

In his old age Eddie's father was given the opportunity to take the lifeboat from the station at Trevose Head to the quayside for Padstow Lifeboat Day. His father was on the wheel and in relaying a message to him from the Mechanic, Eddie referred to him as 'Dad'.

'He looked at me and said: "Don't you call me Dad. You call me Coxswain." So I said, "Well, Coxswain." "That's better," he said. I said, "Want to call the Coastguard and tell them about our ETA [estimated time of arrival]?" And do you know what my Dad said? "Never mind the bloody ETA. You just tell them what time we're gonna get there!"

Janie Thomas, daughter of fisherman Harry Fulfit at Mevagissey, recalled his going out on the lifeboat. 'My father was a youngster when the lifeboat was kept at Portmellon, the next cove from us. The lifeboat was kept on a wagon, and he used to go in the shafts of the wagon. The men used to push, and he steered aright around to go out on the beach and into the water. And he would get wet! The Coxswain said that when he grew up to be a man, he should have a seat on the boat. And he kept his word.

> 'The lifeboat was kept at Mevagissey after the station was built. When it was launched all the women used to go to have a look. 'Twas marvellous really, because there was two or three crew on the station to let her go [down the slipway]. And there was crew up in her, with their oars up, waiting to put them down into the water. And she went swoosh! Down, and out! She'd be halfway out t' the lighthouse time they got them in the water. Then they'd be rowing, and her mast would go up …
>
> 'When the lifeboat boom went, and he had to go, my mother would sit and cry and weep the whole time. Because you see, lifeboats didn't go out often then, unless it was real bad weather, and she was always afraid he wouldn't come back.'

The women provided much needed back-up for their hardy menfolk, many of whom served in the lifeboats in these treacherous waters. 'The old lifeboatmen of Cadgwith were particularly noted for their fearlessness and fine seamanship,' said local fisherman William Arthur. When asked to pinpoint the hazards, William replied: 'As you know, there's a very big reef of rocks, the Staggs. They run out a mile from the Lizard, and around them the water's very shallow. Where you get shallow water you get big breaking seas, and that's the dangerous part of it, and also a strong tide and conflicting tides, one meeting the other, and that throws up a big sea.'

The lifeboatmen of Cadgwith had a very distinguished record of service, going to the aid of a variety of vessels, saving hundreds of lives and receiving awards for outstanding seamanship and gallantry. This included the epic, all-time recordbreaking service to the White Star liner *Suevic*, which ran on the Maenheere Reef off the Lizard in foggy conditions in March 1907.

'My father was the 2nd Coxswain when the *Suevic* came in, and they landed 227 from her,' said William.

'He became the Coxswain after that. My brother Buller, he was in the lifeboat for most of his life. He was a great character, known all over Cornwall, almost. The pilot gigs are named after him. I went in the lifeboat when I was 17 years of age, and stopped there until 1970. The first one I was in was the *Minnie Moon*. Twelve oars, a bowman and two coxswains. A very big boat for handling in a small place, you see.

'When the maroons were put off, they come running from all quarters, farmers and fishermen all alike. 'Cos it took quite a lot of people to launch the boat. She weighed seven tons, you see, very heavy. Well, you had a long rope on the bow, and all the helpers got hold of this rope and pulled her down the beach on skids. Round timbers were laid on the beach about 10 ft apart, and you had a man with a big pot of grease, greasing them all the way down. The whole crew would get in the lifeboat, and you'd have your oars up straight, so when you got into the water you were ready to strike off. The lifeboat often got washed back. Then you had to pull her back up the beach and try again. Two or three attempts, sometimes, to get her out. When it's low water, it's very shallow.

'The parson, Harry Vyvyan, was the Honorary Secretary of the lifeboat and I remember one Sunday night, everybody was in church and the maroons went up in the middle of the service. And he says, "I'm afraid we have to go", and the parson and everybody else bolted out of the church and came down here. The parson often went out in the boat, you see. He was Cornish, born at the Lizard, and spent most of his time in boats down at Church Cove, when he was a youngster.

'They were all rowing and sailing boats, no engines then. When the crew got wet – which we did in an open boat, no cabins like they got now – you felt pretty miserable. But people were hardier, brought up to these conditions.

'We used to have big leather boots – had to keep putting dubbin on them. We'd have sou'westers in bad weather, and long, very heavy oilskins. The lifejackets in the old days were made of cork, and they were very cumbersome things. Awful for rowing in. Beautiful stuff they wear now, to what we had. And they don't have to row, you see.'

The oars were of paramount importance in the open lifeboats, and they carried spares. Even so, emergencies sometimes arose. 'You couldn't do anything if you lost your oars. The Cadgwith lifeboat went to a wreck down off the Lizard one time, and she got in under the quarter – the stern of the ship – and broke off several of her oars. Well, she was helpless, pretty well. The Lizard lifeboat was there at the same time, and they passed over their spare oars.'

These lifeboatmen were frequently out for hours on end, and I asked William about provisions at sea:

'Used to have a quart bottle of rum, that was the main thing! There was biscuits, dry, hard biscuits, chocolate, and corned beef kept in a special box in the lifeboat. And you had demijohns full of water for drinking; one of those narrow-necked bottles cased in wicker with wickerwork handles. About five gallons, I suppose. But the rum, that was the main thing.

'The regulations were that you had to be out at sea for six hours before you was allowed to drink the grog. But I don't think they always waited six hours!' William smiled as he cast his mind back to the time he served in Falmouth's Watson Class motor lifeboat. 'The Coxswain, Charlie Brown, he used to drink it every time he went out on practice. Empty the bottle each time! A quart bottle of rum for the whole crew. I remember the lifeboat went out just before Christmas, and of course Charlie got the bottle out, you see. We all had a drink, then Charlie said to the Motor Mechanic, a little chap, we used to call him Titch – "Here you are, Titch, here's yours." And he said, "Oh, I think I'll take mine home, for to put 'en in the Christmas puddin'." Charlie said, "Bugger the Christmas puddin'! If you can't drink 'en, I can. Give 'en here." And down he went!

'We used to think a lot of the lifeboat. Always did. Had complete confidence in her.' I asked if he was ever frightened. 'Well, I don't know,' he replied. 'No, I don't think so. 'Cos we were fishermen. Nothing new to us to be knocked about a bit. Just keep calm, and not get wound up about anything.'

How was the lifeboat rehoused after a service, I wondered?

'Quite easy to get the boat up,' William said. 'Had a big winch at the end of the lifeboat-house and winched it up with that. Almost 20 people on the handles, I suppose. Then the boat had to be washed down and cleaned. We had a hose in the house and just washed her down. That was my job very often when my father was Coxswain. Everything was put in place ready to go again.

'When the lifeboatmen, who were all fishermen, returned from sea, we all went to the pub, then called the Cadgwith Hotel, and had a pint. That was the main centre of the village – still is. What did we talk about? Oh, fishing, mostly. We would talk about wrecks and characters – all sorts. But mostly about the sea and our lives at sea.' William summed up his life in Cadgwith by saying: 'Could've done with a bit more money sometimes. But it's been happy and healthy. When you go to sea, it's a healthy life.'

Chapter 10

Fishermen at War

The coastal community was always wary of seaborne attack, and the situation of war had a particular impact on the local seafarers, whose boats might be requisitioned, and who might be pressed into service with the Navy where their seafaring skills were recognised.

In the First World War the bigger Cornish ports became bases for naval operations. Battleships, submarines, captured German vessels and decoy vessels occupied Falmouth Haven, the traditional haunt of the oystermen, and there were food shortages and restrictions on the movements of the local boatmen. The port of Falmouth was responsible for organising and regrouping the convoys of merchant shipping for the provision of essential supplies. 'Coast watchers' maintained a vigil from the shore, as at Penare Point near Mevagissey, where elderly fishermen fulfilling this role were protected from wind and rain by half of an upturned yacht called the *Saucy Nell*.

The Second World War brought the danger of attack from the air as well as by sea, and the civilian population was now at risk.

Mines were laid along the shore and the beaches were cordoned off with scaffold-like structures, coils of barbed wire and anti-tank defences. It was official policy that fishermen should be earmarked for service at sea, either in the Navy or in their normal occupation because of their vital role in food production, and that they should continue fishing until they were required for naval service.

With the outbreak of war in 1939, the larger Cornish ports resumed their emergency naval role, with movements of British ships, including fishing vessels, under the control of the Admiralty. Netted booms were placed across harbour entrances, with armed guards in sentry boxes at the end of piers. Entry to the harbours and other prohibited areas was by permit or variable passwords.

The biggest and most efficient boats were requisitioned for naval service, and the black-out situation, by land and sea, with the dimming or extinguishing of navigational lights, led to very restricted periods for fishing, particularly during the winter. Vessels were not permitted to be underway at night within three miles of the coast for security reasons, and thus the smaller boats were compelled to get back to port before sunset and remain until sunrise. Fishing was a very risky business, for apart from the usual seafaring hazards there was the constant threat of enemy action from aircraft and submarines, as well as the danger of the minefields laid by German destroyers to hamper the vital shipping movements. Requisitioned trawlers, which took part in minewatching, passed the information on to minesweepers, with maps being made of the clearance channels.

Falmouth boatman Leonard Morrison, whose boat and expertise were harnessed for wartime service, was engaged in a variety of highly dangerous activities, including mine-laying work around Falmouth and the Helford river.

'They were all electric, and I carried the heads of the mines in on the beach. They had a little coaster called the *Cornish Coast*, I shall never forget her. Well, 'ee used to drop the mines over and I used to follow in and take the heads of

*Curtis's Shipyard, Polean, Looe in November 1939, where fire floats
and other craft were being constructed for emergency use.
(George Ellis Collection, Cornish Studies Library)*

the mines and take them in to Middle Point, to where they
could be set off at any time. And down Helford, just the
same. We had two lots of different sized mines in Falmouth
Harbour, but Helford only had one string of one size. One
time I was moored to something in a certain position and
the *Cornish Coast* came right into me. Stove in my side. I
didn't sink or anything but I was out of action for a few
days, thank God!

'The Membly Hall was the head base. That was Fort 1,
but I was with Fort 4, up over Taylor's Garage. If they
wanted a boat or anything at all afloat, they'd arrange it
at Fort 4. There was always a duty officer, a Wren and a
watchman on all night. I remember when two of my mates
were landing a high-ranking naval officer from somewhere
or other. Well, they didn't knock the engine out, and it

came right in, hit the quay and over the officer went on his back. A naval officer stretched out in the bottom of the boat! He reported 'en and they were locked up. Next morning they were detained as they were about to leave work, but they were released a few hours later, because they were still civilians, you see. They had to explain, and to tell you the truth they'd had a little drop too much!'

Leonard was also involved with the emplacement of decoy landing craft upriver, which had been constructed at Turnaware Bar, where he was summoned at short notice.

'It was very secretive; I couldn't even tell my wife where I was going. These craft they were building were only dummy, with 40-gallon barrels to keep them afloat. They looked like MTS landing craft. You never heard so much noise in your life when they come down the slipway. Nobody said nothing. The first you'd know was "Oh, she's away" and boom! boom! boom! coming down the slipway. Once they were afloat we had to grab them and find the buoys to moor them to. We knew what they were for. We knew that they were put there so that any German planes sent over to take photographs would take them for real.'

Falmouth had been bombed in the early part of the war and the river was a highly sensitive area. Boatman Peter Newman was born at Smugglers Cottage, Tolverne, which was commandeered as a nerve centre for operations in the build-up to D-Day. He told me,

'The river used to be lit up on occasions because the Jerries would come over during the day, see Truro, plot it, then return at night to bomb it. They used to black-out Truro and light up parts of the river. They used to tow decoy ships around which were made out of canvas and drums. My

father was involved in this with his pleasure boats. He used
to tow around these barges or assist other boats to do it.'

Even before the Americans got involved in the war there was what
was known as the River Patrol, which was like the Home Guard
but only for the river. Rodney Newman and his boat were a
familiar part of the wartime river scene. However, one night, after
he had spoken to one of the Patrol, they challenged him with
flashing lights, fired two warning shots and demanded to see his
permits!

John Cockle, a seaman from Truro, took up the theme.

'In the early days of the war, when the River Patrol Home
Guard was hurriedly set up, the harbour came under the
Corporation. Old Dick Rowe of Malpas who worked for
the Truro Harbourmaster was telling me about it. They
were issued with cheese-cutter hats and Navy battledress,
instead of the usual khaki, and given old Ross rifles. The
commandeered boats were fitted out with the old Lewis
machine guns as their anti-aircraft defence. Well, Dick
Rowe told me as how they saw this plane with lights, and
assumed it was one of ours. It carried on up the river,
turned back, then came downriver with the front gunner
firing at them. "Did you open up with the Lewis gun?" I
asked. "Not bloody likely," says Dick, "they was firing at
we!"'

It was deemed necessary for local boats around the coast to be
armed, and fishermen, lifeboatmen and others took gunnery
courses at the emergency naval bases. These boats were
encouraged to move around in convoys. Travelling lifeboat
mechanic Jack Snell explained,

'You had to be armed in case you picked up a German
airman who was himself armed. The Admiralty had to be
notified of the movements of local boats.'

There were occasions when amateur attempts at warfare backfired, as when the Belgian crew of the Porthleven fishing vessel *Boy George* took aim at a marauding enemy plane – and shot down their own mast.

The depleted number of fishing boats, frequently undermanned, led to a shortage of fish and price controls. This put an emphasis on imported products such as dried and salted cod, snoek and whale meat, which were unpopular with the public. According to the Ministry of Agriculture and Fisheries: 'Throughout nearly the whole course of the war the fishing industry, in contradiction to other food producing industries, was fighting a battle for existence.'

After the Germans invaded Denmark in April 1940 the Danish fishing vessels in British ports were seized, as it was technically an enemy country. As the war spread, refugees from Holland, Belgium and France fled to this country in fishing vessels. About two-thirds of these were requisitioned for naval purposes, while the remainder were encouraged to fish under licence from ports on the South and West coasts. They were assembled in Dartmouth. The Dutch were ordered to Falmouth, while Belgian vessels were allocated to Brixham, Newlyn and Milford Haven, with the larger ones going to Fleetwood, Cardiff and Swansea. Some of the Belgians who found refuge in Brixham, moved on to Mevagissey when that Devon port was being prepared as an invasion base in 1943.

Military personnel had appeared around Mevagissey at the beginning of the war, when a Home Guard unit was set up. The port came under the control of three naval officers, with the Harbour Office serving as the headquarters. The men were issued with rifles, which could be fired through apertures excavated in the harbour wall, backed up with a machine gun kept in the old lifeboat house. Coastal defences were erected along the shore with sentries at various points, for this was a sensitive area between the naval bases of Plymouth and Falmouth. A large net was placed across the harbour entrance, and fishing was restricted to an area ten miles south of the Dodman and ten miles south-west of Looe.

Some of the fishermen took part in minesweeping activities, and the fleet was alerted to be on standby at the evacuation of Dunkirk in 1940, and the fall of France.

Local fisherman Henry Johns could recall the war years in Mevagissey:

'They had minefields out there, and there was restrictions on fishing. They had a big wire net up across the quay head here, wire with a square mesh. Heaved 'en up with a winch on the quay, see. And if it was pulled up nobody couldn't get in nor out. They used to leave 'en up, so that nothing couldn't get in here by night.

'There was three sailors in charge of the harbour, and one of them was the head man, Leading Seaman. You had to go and get your orders before you went out, and you had to have a permit. They gave you instructions as to how far you was a-going. There was minefields out there and you'd be notified where they was to. And when you was going out, they'd give you a letter to flash for the light, a different letter each night. You had a certain time to come in and when you came in by night, you had a letter – you would flash your torch and they would let 'un in. If you couldn't show a letter, they wouldn't let 'en in; they'd think "Well, may be a foreigner", see?

'They done a lot of filming round the harbour, 1944 – *Johnny Frenchman* – very good film, that was. I can remember a boat used by the filming company called the *Maris Stella*, a French crabber, she was. They hired she from down Newlyn. One day we was coming in from crabbing in our boat, the *Pet*, and this ole boat was sailing in, you know, just for a scene for the cameras, and we come in together. And when we'd come ashore, Harry Mills, a chap from Mevagissey who was working for the film party said, "'Ere, thanks, 'Enry, for looking after the *Maris Stella*." I told him we was coming in at the same time, but he kept going on and on. "'Ere's ten bob a man for 'ee," he said. So we had ten bob a man – and we never knew he was in trouble! His engine had broken down!'

During the First World War the much acclaimed boatbuilder Percy Mitchell had been an apprentice at the yard of Roberts & Co in Mevagissey, which had been engaged in constructing vessels for the Admiralty. During the Second World War he resumed this role from his boatyard in neighbouring Portmellon, producing 'Vindictive' pattern fog floats, diesel-engined motor cutters, motor fishing vessels (MFVs) and ships' lifeboats for the Admiralty, and 14-ft dories for the War Office. Some of his former workers were constructing large wooden minesweepers at Par for Messrs Curtis of Looe. He was instructed to liaise with the Coastguards and report anything suspicious. Over 30 years later, in September 1978, the area's wartime Naval link was strengthened when Mevagissey adopted the Sea Fisheries' Protection vessel, HMS *Stubbington*.

Mevagissey in September 1944, where the filming of Johnny Frenchman *took place. The boat CM4703 is the* Maris Stella, *which had escaped from the Llede Sein across the Channel to Newlyn in June 1940. She continued to fish from Newlyn throughout the war years. (George Ellis Collection, Cornish Studies Library)*

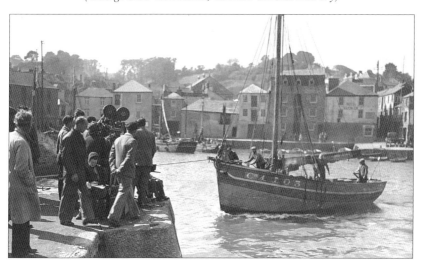

An Admiralty MFV being launched from Percy Mitchell's yard at Portmellon during the Second World War. (Original sketch by Jenny Fryatt)

Newlyn, like other ports on the Channel coast, absorbed an influx of French and Belgian refugees in the early part of the war, and others arrived from the Channel Islands ahead of the German advance. The Belgian trawlers which had not been requisitioned continued to work out of Newlyn, and East Coast trawlers were also a familiar sight in the harbour. Before the outbreak of war there had been a plan to divert these fishing vessels to West Coast ports if that area fell victim to enemy attacks. Although it had not been necessary to implement these measures, there had been a gradual shift westwards.

Cornwall, which became increasingly vulnerable when the Germans reached the French Channel coast, was the scene of incredible, highly dangerous secret operations involving requisitioned Belgian and Breton vessels. They were repainted to resemble Breton fishing boats, with iron filings added to the paint to create a shabby, workaday appearance, and equipped with authentic-looking sails and flags. Those aboard were got up to resemble Breton fishermen, thus allowing the craft and her crew to blend in with the fishing fleet around the coast of Brittany.

The groups carrying out these covert operations were the Free

French, operating out of Mylor, the Secret Intelligence Service (SIS) working from Falmouth, and the Special Operations Executive (SOE) based on the Helford river. Their objectives were to help shot-down airmen and prisoners of war to escape to Britain, to gather intelligence behind enemy lines, and carry out acts of sabotage and cause disruption in German-held territory. The skills required to navigate the hazardous coasts of Cornwall and Brittany, the two-way trafficking of people and the ingenious methods devised to convey messages and land equipment are reminiscent of the great days of smuggling.

Enlisted local fishermen took part in some of the secret operations, including the Stevenson family, who were an established part of the quayside scene at Newlyn. William Stevenson said that his Uncle Bryan was involved with the paperwork, and attended meetings with naval personnel at the Ferryboat Inn at Helford Passage. He recalled some of the local fishermen being suspicious of the converted vessels ostensibly fishing out of Newlyn, and heard rumours about the presence of German spies in the port, as had been the case in the First World War.

As D-Day approached, the coastal communities became aware of heightened military activity by land and sea, much of it centred around the Fal and Helford areas. As marine artist Tony Warren put it,

'Things were beginning to build up for Operation Overlord. They built 'hards' along the waterfront; there was masses of gear everywhere. You couldn't move for jeeps and military vehicles. Ships and landing craft all over the place. The entire Moors down there was completely and utterly filled up with tents as far as you could see, and there was an immense great marquee outside the post office with all the telephone lines connected up into the system. You couldn't believe it! And then suddenly they'd go away. Suddenly overnight they were all gone. The place was cleared. Then next morning, they were back again. On manoeuvres. Did that two or three times. Then they went, and Falmouth suddenly became quiet again.'

Claudie Richards of Polruan had vivid memories of his wartime service for the Navy in his requisitioned boat, *Rosemary*.

'The Navy took her over just before the war broke out in 1939. Well, they took the mast out – she had a mast leaning back over and you could hoist a sail, and of course when she was fishing it was necessary to have a mizzen on her to keep her head to the wind when you was pulling

your nets or lines. So all that was taken out of her. The cushions was taken out from when she was a pleasure boat, and she was painted grey instead of white. She used to have a badge on the bow, which was a flag with a spray of the flower rosemary in it, red background with blue around it, and then her name. She always looked very nice.' A faraway look came into his eyes, and he chuckled fondly at the recollection.

Initially the Navy harnessed Claudie's knowledge of these waters, and he told me of instances which relied on his experience and instinct. 'One afternoon Cap'n Perryman's

Claudie Richards in 1940 when he was an RNLI Travelling Mechanic. (Paul Richards)

daughter, a Wren – we called her Lollipop – come to me and she said, "Claudie, you gotta come up to the office right away." So I said, "All right, Lollipop." And I went down there, and Cap'n Perryman said to me, "Claude, would you go to sea and meet a submarine?" I said, "Yes, if you'll tell me where to go."

'But it was in, like, naval language. It was all degrees on the compass and I didn't like to say "I've never steered on degrees, always on points". So I asked Commander Pritchard, "I wonder if you'd be kind enough, sir, to write that down for me?" 'Yes, certainly, Claude," he said. "That's south-east to the east, half east." I said, "Thank you, sir." So he said, "Now then, when you come back?" I said, "Nor'-west to west, half west." "Yes, that's right," he said, "you go out and do that, nine miles."

'And I was going out, and it was dark, with patches of drizzly rain. So I sniffed and sniffed again, and I thought, that's cigarette smoke. *Rosemary* would do about six miles an hour, so I slowed the engine down, then it come calm and I could smell the cigarette smoke. Then suddenly this great thing loomed up in front of me – it was the conning tower of a submarine!

'I went alongside and this officer called out, "I say, how did you find me?" "It's your cigarette smoke!" He says, "What?" I said, "I could smell your cigarettes. I don't smoke meself and I can smell them." "Well I'm damned!" he said. And he was a Lieutenant Commander, I think; from what I could see of him he had two half rings. He was the skipper of the submarine, anyhow.

'So I brought two gentlemen and a lady ashore, but I didn't see that lady. She was in a bad way. She was all wrapped up and lying down in the boat. I got an idea she'd been beaten up. So I started reversing me course, and on the way back to Fowey, *Rosemary* suddenly lifted up in the air, really solid, and down. Then I heard, splash! I thought, I wonder what that is? Well, I landed these people down to the Town Quay. It was troops and all down there, and the girl was took away in an ambulance. Then I had orders to proceed to the office.'

Claudie Richards aboard his passenger boat, Rosemary, *in 1979. It was named after his much loved fishing boat, which was requisitioned by the Admiralty in the Second World War. (Paul Richards)*

The Officer in Charge was amazed to hear about the giveaway aroma of cigarettes, and thanked him for passing on this useful information. When he described the sudden disturbance of water that caused *Rosemary* to rise up in the air, he was told, 'That's mine laying, Claudie.'

'He showed me a chart,' said Claudie, 'and the next day they had minesweepers out and exploded eight German mines!'

The Admiralty was wont to call on Claudie's services at any time of the day or night. Sometimes he could be away for prolonged periods, ferrying duty officers across the water, and picking them up in the middle of the night.

When the war was over the requisitioned boats gradually returned to their home ports, having been reconverted and reconditioned. Monetary payments were made in lieu of vessels lost. Some of the MFVs constructed by the Admiralty were adapted for peacetime use and made available for purchase by tender, with priority given to those whose boats had been lost in wartime service. W. Stevenson & Sons of Newlyn took this opportunity to build up the size of their fishing fleet. A welcome realisation was that reduced fishing activity during the wartime years had given the fish stocks the opportunity to replenish themselves.

Chapter 11

The Charm of Polperro

The ancient fishing port of Polperro, immortalised in literature and art, has delighted generations of visitors with its beautiful workaday charms. Polperro, with limited access overland, has always lived by its fishing, and the proud, close-knit community remained relatively isolated for centuries.

In 2009, when Looe fisherman Alan Dingle was recalling some of the colourful characters he had encountered around the coast in the years following the Second World War, he remarked: 'Of course, all the fishermen back then had a very strong Cornish accent. And if you went to Polperro, which was only four miles away, you couldn't understand what they were talking about! They were so *broad*!' He went on, 'There was a lot of characters down there. I used to know quite a lot of them when I was young, 'cos my father was well in with the Polperro fishermen. We were all pilcharding together, like, on the pilchard boats.'

Sitting by the harbourside in the pleasant autumn sunshine, Old Timer Bill Cowan drew my attention to a plaque on a granite seat across the harbour commemorating his father-in-law, Jack Joliffe.

Polperro Inner Harbour in 1914 (Royal Institution of Cornwall)

'He was Harbour Master here for 20 years,' he said. 'Jacko, they used to call him. The Joliffes, they go back generations, fishing. They had a boat called the *Maggie*, I think she was a 21 or 25 ft sailing smack. She is up-country somewhere and they're looking for her now, because one of his grandsons, he'd like to bring her back and see her restored.

'The old fishermen were very superstitious. I used to fish with a lot of them in Plymouth before the war. Underground greyhounds [rabbits],' he chuckled, 'you never talked about them! And the worst thing in the world was to see a vicar or a preacher coming down to the quay. They'd turn around and go home again. They'd go home, sit on a chair, wait for five or ten minutes, and pray that he'd gone by the time they come down again.

'The Puckeys was another fishing family. They used to say at one time, if you ever come in, no matter what time of the day or night, and there wasn't a Puckey there, just go away. They used to wait for the boats to come in. When we was pilchard fishing we'd come in at two, three, four o'clock – all depends where the fishing was, and there'd be one or two Puckeys walking up and down the quay in the middle of the night. And don't forget there weren't no electric lights here then! 'Twas all Tilley lamps. And they'd come to us and want to know if you wanted a hand to land, to earn five or ten shillings, They were on the lookout for a job, you know, to earn a shilling or two. They were semi-retired, like, a generation ahead of us at the time.

'Another character seen on the quayside just after the war was Reuben Oliver, the harbour master. I remember him very well. He'd lost his left arm in the 1914 war. First of all he was a clerk, and did all the clerking and the writing and that for the harbour, and then they combined the two jobs. He was also a magistrate, and an approachable and knowledgeable man. People used to go to him for help and advice. Polperro was becoming very popular with the holidaymakers, and this little village was the first in Cornwall to have restrictions on cars coming into it. We used to get issued with permits to stick in your car window to say that you lived here, to come back into the village in summertime.'

Bill is Polperro's sole remaining, and much cherished, Old Timer, and a familiar figure around the quayside. He told me:

'I was born on the Barbican in Plymouth, where my family were fishermen, and I started fishing with them when I was 14. When I came back after the war, things had altered, and I couldn't really settle. Then I had a chance to go aboard a pilchard fishing boat in Newlyn. It was one of Shippam's boats – Shippam's, the paste people. So I caught a train from Plymouth with me fishing gear, and went down to Newlyn.

'As I walked down the quay one of the fishermen shouted from his boat, "What are you doing here?" This was the *Patsy Anne*, and he was the skipper, Frank Oliver. He used to come to Plymouth fishing quite a lot, and we knew 'em, like. I told him I'd got a berth aboard a fishing boat, so he said, "I'm one short, come with me. Polperro is a lot nearer to Plymouth than what Newlyn is, and you could go home for weekends." So I shipped with him. We was a crew of five hands, and we went pilchard fishing and long line fishing. We used to do, like, 24-hour trips in the Channel, long lining; we'd shoot eight to nine miles of line. The *Patsy Anne* was 41 ft 6 inches. She was a St Ives gig-built boat, very good boat, she was. Frank Oliver, who named her after one of his daughters, was a very hardworking man, one of the cleverest men that ever sailed out of this port. He had the *Patsy Anne* for many years, and when he eventually sold her I bought my own boat.

'I bought her from Margate. She was 36 ft, she was, and only six or seven years old. She was called the *Winston Churchill* when I bought her, and I changed the name to the *Westward*, because I was born in the west, and my course was nearly all west. And I carried on fishing here. I had one crew with her, like. We used to do mackerel fishing, then. I've done a bit of trawling and scalloping, all from here. I was 65 when I sold her, and I got a smaller boat then, just for pleasure, for taking people down the coast, giving them a talk, a yarn. She was one of those little 21-ft boats, and called the *Lowena*. That means joy and happiness in Cornish.

'One time when I was out shark fishing from Looe, I had a young gentleman who was eager to go out sharking with me. 'Twas the first time he'd ever done anything like that. We'd been having a yarn coming down the river, but when we was going out to sea, he said, "Is it going to be like this?" It wasn't *bad* weather, just a little fresh wind, like. I said, "Yeah, this is what it's like. You make your mind up.

Bill Cowan (centre) with his mates, Dick Joliffe and Wilfred Puckey.
(Bill Cowan & Polperro Heritage Museum of Smuggling and Fishing)

If I take you back now, I can get someone else. But if you go further than Looe Island and want me to stop, I loses me day's work." He said, "I couldn't stick this all day. I'll give you twice as much as a day's wages, if you will only take me back!" I thought it was quite funny. It wasn't as if it had been *bad* weather with big waves. But he weren't gonna have that!'

We paused to savour the atmosphere of the inner harbour at low tide, where sea birds were foraging in the mud, and boats were being supported on legs or cradles to keep them upright.

'We're a half-tide harbour,' Bill explained. 'With your long rubber seaboots on, you can get aboard them with a ladder. In Polperro at this moment, we've got 13 fishing

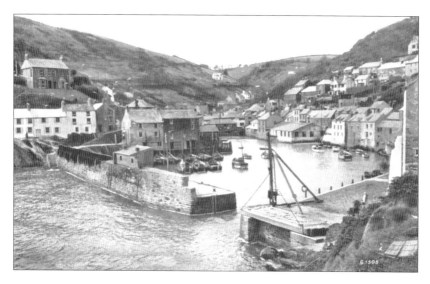

Polperro harbour in the 1950s. (Sheila Bird Collection)

boats. We've got four trawlers away to sea. They all belong alongside the quay.

'The fishing has changed with all these rules and regulations. When I came back after the war, the idea was to take a bit of grub with you, and go out and catch as much as you could, when you could. But today – you can't do this, you can't do that. It is very restrictive.

'One thing that happened on the *Patsy Anne* when we went on a long-lining trip – that's usually 24, 48 hours, like – caused quite a stir. In they days we went to sea with just a compass and a clock. An alarm clock. No sophisticated navigational equipment. No radio. You'd steer by the compass and set the alarm clock to go off at a certain time, and then you'd know you were up to your fishing ground. We used to put a dan every two and a half miles (dans – that's marker buoys with weights on and a flag on top to show where the line is).

'Well, we went away in the back of the Eddystone and

caught pilchards for bait, and the weather wasn't too bad at all. We started to shoot the long line, which was eight miles long, putting in the dans, and it started getting foggy. But we carried on shooting, and when we got to the far end the fog was coming in really thick. So we turned around and Frank Oliver, the skipper, he reversed the course and started picking up the dans. Anyhow, we got our distance, but couldn't find the last one. We tied a rope to the last but one, dropped a rope with a hook on, which was 120 fathoms when it's out, and 'e sunk to the bottom. And we laid to that.

'We was there 24 hours. It was hair-raising. When you've got thick fog like that you hear sounds, and no two people aboard the boat'll agree where it comes from. We was in the shipping lane and there was steamers going up and down, passing, and their foghorns going, and their wash would come … When a little bit of the dawn came up the next day, we looked out and saw the dan we'd been looking for, about a couple of hundred yards away from us. So we picked 'en up right away, and started to work. Frank wasn't going to leave his line there, because to lose your means of getting a living was the last thing a fisherman wants.

'We didn't get a lot of fish. We'd been out too long and it'd been damaged. Well, by now we'd been missed. And the cry went up, "The boat's overdue, 24 hours overdue!" And shipping was asked to keep a look out. We never had no radio set, nor nothing at all. When we'm up past the Start [Point] and on course for Polperro, we seen a merchant ship outside of us. It was one of Everard's china clay ships; he was going up channel and we was coming down. He changed course and when he come past us, he didn't stop or nothing, and they all waved. So we just waved back.

'But he reported that he'd spotted *Patsy Anne*, and he could see four hands aboard. Now this caused a hue and cry, because we was five in the crew, and they thought there was one missing. The other one was having a nap, because he'd been on watch all the time. Anyrate, when we got in the tide was out, so we tied up to the buoys outside. And all the cliffs were lined with people, hundreds of people, to see this missing fishing boat come in that had been missing for two days. Frank, he said, "I'm not going in with all they people there. We'll wait till it gets dark." And when the tide came in, it was dark,' chuckled Bill, adding, 'That was in the very early Fifties, that was.'

Sadly, not all such alerts have been concluded with sighs of relief in this close-knit fishing community, and Bill cited the case of the FV *Clair* in 1982. 'I think she was netting and there was two hands aboard, Mike Faulkner, he was the skipper, and Roger Davies. She was picked up by another Looe boat and they went aboard her. The engine was still running, but there was no sign of the crew. They thought that one might've fallen overboard, and the other went over to save him, but that was an assumption. Their names are on the plaque on the quay in Looe. They was both Polperro men.'

We talked then about the practical humanitarian role quietly maintained by the Fishermen's Mission when tragedy strikes – their ability to remain in touch with fishing families, and their provision of a relaxed and friendly environment in which to get together on a daily basis. 'Fishermen like to stick with fellow fishermen, because they've all got something in common, haven't they? When we were pilcharding out of Newlyn we used to use the Fishermen's Mission. Very good people down there. They go and help the families, these missionary people, you know, come to see you, to have a yarn, like, and they're always welcome. Keeps you in touch with what's going on. 'Tis very nice.'

Chapter 12

Historic Looe

Life in the historic port of Looe, with its constricted entrance, has always been governed by the tide. The tide was out, the trawlers were in, and there was much purposeful activity around the quayside as I tuned in to the maritime scene in July 2009. Cheerful shouts and clanging noises were emanating from the vicinity of the fishmarket, while the fishermen were keeping abreast of events in the course of carrying out essential

Luggers from Looe off to the fishing ground. (Sheila Bird Collection)

maintenance work on their equipment. Further down the quay boatman John Friend, who has been a fisherman for 40 years or so, was standing by his noticeboard keeping visitors informed about the trips on offer when the tide allowed.

John told me that he came from a fishing family and was related to the Pengellys, who have been a part of waterfront life for generations. 'My first skipper was Frank Pengelly, who was known as "Moogie". He was probably the most respected – well, one of the most respected – fishermen in Cornwall.'

I was to hear Moogie's name mentioned many times in the course of my adventures around the harbourside. Having been born in 1920 and learned his craft from the tough breed who had toiled aboard the old sailing boats, he emulated them and had a reputation for working his crew very hard. And he would quietly utter the words, 'God speed the plough', in the traditional way as they shot their nets.

Nobody seemed to know the significance of (Thomas) Frank Pengelly's nickname, but it was pointed out that his father Tom had also been called Moogie. John threw more light on this local tradition:

> 'Because of all the Pengellys here in Looe, they all had their nicknames else you wouldn't know them apart. Like Aubrey John Pengelly was "AJ", who used to own the boat called *Our Daddy*, and there was Bill "Pye" and all his brothers – all the "Pye" Pengellys. And of course a lot of them had the same Christian name. It was all nicknames here in Looe. There was Tiddler Sammels, who was on the *Iris* with Frank Pengelly, and another chap called Billy Fireout, and one called Spaker. My father-in-law was called Oppidy.'

John has great respect for the Old Timers.

> 'They always seemed to know what they were doing, and where they were going. They went by instinct. I remember

going away from here one time, and it was a beautiful morning. We got out near Looe Island, then all of a sudden Frank (Moogie) turned the boat around. We said, "What's the matter?" And he said, "We're going home, boys." We said, "What's the matter? It's a beautiful, fine morning." He said, "Well, I can see the Lizard Light looming." And within an hour and a half, we had a south-easterly gale! All those old sayings, like "Wind before rain, head for home again", they were nearly always right. They were all characters in the old days – or seemed to be.' Then he chuckled. 'But I suppose they'd call me an old character now!'

John outlined his experiences fishing out of Looe.

'When I was at school I used to go summer pilcharding in my holiday. They used to do pilchard fishing at night and shark fishing during the day. I went into fishing in the 1970s, when it was coming up to the height of the mackerel fishing in Cornwall. We used to fish mainly down at Falmouth Bay in those days.'

He emphasised the importance of knowledge of the local waters, and pinpointed navigational hazards, including the Ranney Reef off Looe Island.

'You always go by the rock formations, you know. Between here and what we call the Hore Stone, all the rocks go towards the land, and from Hore Stone down to Polperro, the rocks lean towards the sea. There's little things like that.
    'I've been trawling and long lining and drift netting. Trawling's lovely, easy work.'

A number of trawlers were tied up alongside as we spoke, mostly owned by skippers and families in this picturesque little port, with its intimate, friendly atmosphere. The trawlers were smaller than those to be seen in Newlyn, which are mostly company-owned and spending longer periods at sea. As John pointed out,

> 'Looe is a tidal harbour, and that determines more or less the draught and the size of boats that are here.
>
> 'When we went trawling first, you had to shoot the trawl over the side of the boat. Now, 'tis all stern trawling. We had to shoot the trawl from the side and then keep going round to starboard, so that you didn't drag the trawl into your propeller. Then you had to shoot your sprag – that's the term for the height of your trawl – and that sprag goes to your dan lines to your trawl boards. You gotta shoot them away, and in some conditions with the wind and the tide or whatever, the darned board wouldn't go away properly, and you could be there ages. But with stern trawlers, everything is shot out over the stern, and it all goes away very clean. Very easy. How it never evolved sooner than it did, I don't know.
>
> 'The trawlers were 40 ft or so, with a crew of three. We would have to work around the tides. But you probably had an 18 hour day, and sometimes you were away 36 hours.' He smiled when I asked about the eating and sleeping arrangements. 'Oh, no! You didn't have that sort of thing. No such luxury as that! You were lucky if you had a hot drink all the time you were out.'
>
> 'You steamed out and shot away your trawl, and that would be your rest time. Once you hauled your trawl, your time was taken up with gutting and cleaning, washing and stowing everything. It would all have to be boxed up.'

John nodded in the direction of the fishmarket.

> 'There's lots of fish buyers here. It's all packed up then carted away to different places.'

'As frozen fish?' I asked, somewhat naïvely.

'No! No! It's day-caught fish. There's no frozen fish here in Looe! Maybe down in Newlyn, where the boats are out for two or three weeks, but we pride ourselves on our day-caught fish here!

'When I was out drift fishing,' John went on, 'there was a boat called *Chichester Lass*. She worked out of Newlyn and she was owned by Old Man Shippam. Bobby Jewell was the skipper and he was a Porthleven chap. Mr Shippam was a devout Christian and he wouldn't allow anything that was landed on a Sunday to go through his factory. And when they were at sea, Bobby and his crew used to sing hymns over the radio in four-part harmony. Beautiful. The fishermen were always singing.'

Harold Mutton, conductor of the Looe Fishermen's Choir, with some of the members on the quayside in 1940. (George Ellis Collection, Cornish Studies Library)

Having noticed the rich and pleasing tone of John's voice as soon as we met, I was not altogether surprised to learn that he has long been associated with local choirs.

'There was a fishermen's choir here in Looe. And because Looe had a fishermen's choir, Polperro had to have one too! The choir used to sing in chapels and halls all over the country – we've sung in the Albert Hall in London, all over the place. But the Looe choir disbanded many years ago and now I sing in the Polperro choir. At the moment I'm the last fisherman in the fishermen's choir.'

Leaving John and wandering further along the quay, I ran into former fisherman Joe Bussell, now working at the fish market, who continued the themes of trawling and singing.

'We were trawling and mackerel fishing,' he recalled. 'That was a good life – mackerel fishing – because we used to get all the boats from St Ives and Newlyn up to Looe, and then we'd have a sing-song in the pub, the Ship Hotel. The landlady used to put them up for £1 a week, just bed, no breakfast.

'We learned a lot off the old men, wonderful old boys! When they went pilcharding in the old days, they used to go out of an evening and look for the gannets. Great flocks of gannets would circle about in the sky above shoals of fish. Then all of a sudden they would make a vertical dive down into the water. And the old boys used to shoot their nets around where the gannets went down, and lay there for about two or three hours, hoping that all the pilchards would swim into their nets.

'Then when they started to haul their nets, they pulled them in by hand – no machinery back then. And as they're hauling, there's what they called shaking out – shaking the nets to get all the pilchards out on deck. Then if there's not a lot of pilchards, shooting the nets again, you know. It was a hard life. Many years ago, when they came in they used to count the pilchards into baskets, instead of weighing them.'

The scene inside the fish store, where Lionel Bowdler and his son Brian were busy making nets, would have captured the imagination of any artist with its cleverly stowed and colourful array of fishing equipment. Brian looked a bit surprised at that, then laughed, 'It's just work to us!'

Lionel told me,

'I'm a marine engineer by rights, that's my trade, but when I saw which way the Dockyard was going I decided to go fishing. Then I eventually bought my own boat, a 42-ft stern trawler called the *Maret*.'

'She was built in Germany for the Baltic in 1962, so she's the oldest working boat in the port,' added Brian, who is now her skipper.'

Lionel recalled one memorable occasion when he and Brian were working in the boat.

'We had a wartime mine that we towed up, which we had to bring in to shallow waters for the Navy to blow up. That was quite interesting! He had to sit on it all the way in, to stop it from rolling around. When they blew it up, it was exactly like you see in the war films, just a great big mushroom cloud. That was several years ago.

'1994,' said Brian, 'my first year in the lifeboat.'

And as we went on to talk about the Looe lifeboat and the station's interaction with neighbouring lifeboat crews, Lionel pointed out that Brian had been given an award for gallantry. 'For a rescue he did up off Downderry. I'm very proud of him.' I too could remember the events of that terrible night, when two young lives were saved, and added my congratulations.

Chapter 13

From Pilchards to Sharks

Over in West Looe, 81-year-old Alan Dingle recalled his early days, when fishermen occupied the surrounding cottages, and their numerous children played in the Square just below his light and airy flat overlooking the harbour. The waterfront was then the scene of vibrant mercantile activity on both sides of the river.

'I've seen ships coming in here from all over the place – London and all around the coast, and foreign boats,' he said. 'The pilots used to guide them in and out. 'Twas all luggers and herring and pilchard fishing in Looe then; even down to West Looe it was full of luggers. This harbour is tidal, and you had a strong current. If the tide's just started to go out, and there was no wind to sail, all the ladies used to go down on the pier and help pull the boats out of the harbour with ropes. Then the crew would take up their oars to clear the end of Banjo Pier. All this – the women on the pier and everything – it was quite a sight years ago.

'Out in the Channel on a winter's night, I've seen as many as a hundred boats fishing. There'd be boats from Looe, Polperro, Mevagissey, Newlyn... and they'd come down from up the East Coast. There'd be a mass of lights – as big an area as the city of Plymouth. Everybody catching pilchards.

'Before the war all the luggers had sails, then they introduced the engines. My grandfather and uncle that I started with in 1944, they had engines. It made the work a lot easier.

'You have to treat the sea with respect. The men I trained with were very experienced. They knew everything about the area – the weather, the conditions of the sea, and you were told not to do this, and not to do that.' Alan paused, then chuckled. 'We were out there one night when I was a youngster, and I was whistling. The skipper, he said to me, "We got enough wind without you whistling", and he wouldn't let me have no dinner! So I learned my lesson there, quick!'

'The luggers were usually about 44 to 45 ft long, and they all had five bunks in them, below. There was always the skipper, and one was usually the engineer, and the rest were the crew – usually one done all the cooking. You never knew how long you'd be out. It varied. Sometimes in the winter you could shoot your nets at five o'clock and by six o'clock you'd have to pull them in again. You'd be full. Another time you'd have to shoot two or three times, so you wouldn't get back till the morning. When I was pilcharding the wife never knew when I was coming home.

'We had an old iron stove down below, with an oven, and a funnel going up through the deck. It was a lovely, cosy place to go after you'd been fishing in the cold and wet for hours. Take off your oilskins and go down there night-time, with the fire going and all – it was nice. They used to do roast dinners, real roast dinners, stews and all sorts of things like that.'

Alan Dingle at the age of 80 ferrying passengers across to West Looe in his boat, the Sharon. *(Alan & Jeanne Dingle)*

We talked about the role of women in the fishing industry, and of the age-old taboo about women and boats. 'A lot of the fishermen have got some funny customs, and are very superstitious. There have been no women had much to do with fishing in my time. Not commercially, but they used to help out on the quayside, and salt and pack the pilchards, putting them in barrels to be transported to Italy. In the war a lot of women worked in a fish factory up the West Looe river, packing pilchards in tins.

'During the war Looe was a port for the Admiralty. There was a shipyard up the West Looe river, the Curtis and Pape shipyard, where they built the torpedo boats and all the launches for the Navy. All the East Looe quay over there was workshops, from the bridge right down to the Fish Market. A lot of the fishermen were in the Naval Reserve, but there was still some fishing going on. We were not allowed out at night-time. At the end of the war, before I started fishing, I went with my father. We used to go out in the dark, switch the engine off, and drift out the river so they wouldn't see us. Well then, out on the end of West Looe they had searchlights and guns. So the first thing they used to do if they had seen this boat going out, was to switch the searchlight on, and fire the gun across your bows! So you had to turn around and come back again. The army was posted out there, and also the Home Guard. It was a bit like Dad's Army!

'After the war, in the Fifties, the fishermen were glad to see the tourists, for the trade, like. A lot of them had luggers, or small boats, and they took people out on trips. Shark fishing came in in the early Fifties. That was huge and it's still going on. I've done shark fishing for about 45 years or so. There was a chap here called Brigadier Caunter, and he had a small boat called the *Swordfish*. Through being a brigadier, I suspect he'd gone big game fishing out abroad. He used to go out here hoping to catch tuna, but he'd come home with two blue sharks, one on each side of the boat, tied by the tail under the bollard on the stern.

Alan Dingle aboard his boat the Lady Betty *in the late 1950s.*

And everybody laughed at him, see? Until somebody caught on, and thought, "'Ere!"

'That's what started the shark fishing. That turned into Looe becoming the shark headquarters of Great Britain!

'When I started there was about 25 shark boats. We used to bring in the big sharks and have them weighed on the quay. They would hoist them up in the air in front of everybody. There'd be thousands of visitors every night on the quay to watch the sharks being weighed. At that time a lot of the tourist trade was private bookings. Someone would book me for five or six days, sometimes a week. Then it gradually got that we'd take ordinary tourists in threes and fours, and they'd pay so much each. We'd provide all the equipment, bait the lines for them. You'd set the lines out and they would catch it on the rod, then you would get it into the boat. The shark would have to be over 75 lbs before they could apply to join the Shark Club. The fish weren't of any commercial value, or nothing. Later on they put tags on them, and put them back again for research.'

We talked finally of the disappearance of the traditional luggers and the new breed of sailing enthusiasts who recognise the fine quality of the 'good old wooden boats' and have been instrumental in tracking down and restoring the rotting craft with loving care, whatever the cost.

'And now they've all been renovated and done up, and all under new sail. Beautiful! The sails are all colours now. They have the Looe Lugger Races and a lot of the old luggers come back now. That is fantastic!'

Chapter 14

Newlyn – Foremost Fishing Port

The inhabitants of Newlyn, which has emerged as the foremost Cornish fishing port in these difficult times, have always demonstrated their independence, pride and determination, and an ability to adapt to changing circumstances.

A plaque on the wall of the Fishermen's Mission in Newlyn recalls the epic voyage of the lugger *Mystery*, which set sail for Australia on 18th November 1854, reaching Melbourne on 14th March 1855, having accomplished an unparalleled feat of seamanship. Richard Kelynack Cocks, a descendant of crew member Job Kelynack, explained that master carpenter Charles Kelynack had emigrated to Australia, and had fired the imagination of his brother Job and other relatives in his letters home. Job suggested that the family sell their fishing boat *Mystery* to raise the money to pay their fares to go out and join him, but his brother-in-law, Captain Richard Nicholl, who had a Master's ticket, declared that he would navigate their own boat to Australia! Most of the crew eventually returned to this country, including Job Kelynack and Charles Boase, whose descendants Jim and Ben Batten treasured the sextant used on the voyage and wore his gold ring with pride. This great adventure was emulated by the famous seafaring adventurer Pete Goss in a replica boat called the *Spirit of Mystery* in 2008/9.

In the mid-1980s Ben Batten was proud to tell me that his fisherman father, Benjamin Green Batten, was involved in the more domestic seafaring exploit of October 1937, which culminated in the Newlyn long liner *Rosebud* (PZ 87), sailing up the Thames to deliver a petition to Westminster amidst a blaze of publicity. He explained that a dictatorial council's slum clearance scheme, which threatened to sweep away much of picturesque old Newlyn including many fishermen's cottages close to the harbour, had aroused great passion and indignation. He said, 'A committee of fishermen and eminent residents, including the artist Stanhope Forbes, was set up, and hit on this idea in traditional Newlyn style. The *Rosebud* had a great send off, to the encouraging strains of *Fight the good fight*! As it happened, the scheduled demolition was halted by the outbreak of the Second World War, with the buildings being used to house Dutch and Belgian refugees.'

The Spirit of Mystery, *in which maritime adventurer Pete Goss re-enacted the voyage of the* Mystery, *in Williamstown, Melbourne, on 10 March 2009.
(Eric Bird)*

Ben spoke of the port's historical relationship with the Breton and Belgian fishermen and the East Coast steam trawlers, and the emergence of the Stevenson family as leading fish merchants and trawler owners.

'The French crabbers came to Newlyn

for many years,' he mused, conjuring up the evocative aroma of French cigarettes which once wafted across the harbourside. 'In the 1920s they were mostly from Camaret, and lived aboard their vessels. They were unable to speak English, but were fine seamen, and well liked. They used to wander around in clogs, with their hands in the pockets of their much-patched, wide-legged blue trousers, which could be rolled up when they gathered limpets and winkles from the rocks. These fishermen were great ones for snails! They used to go round the local hedgerows looking for snails.' When the war broke out, Belgian and other refugees who were familiar with Newlyn as a port of call arrived here in their boats, with little more than what they stood up in.

Many of the trawlers were requisitioned by the Admiralty, while the remaining boats continued to operate under wartime restrictions. The banning of night fishing was resented by some, who regarded it as a serious blow to the pilchard industry, and felt they should have been consulted. Sadly, Ben Batten lost his father in a fishing tragedy in Mount's Bay in 1941.

The East Coast trawlers which had become part of the Newlyn scene had developed steam power early on, and this had set the trend

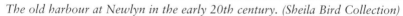

The old harbour at Newlyn in the early 20th century. (Sheila Bird Collection)

A fish seller of Newlyn demonstrates her wares in the early 20th century. (Cornish Studies Library)

for larger deep sea vessels with a much wider scope. Stevenson built up their fleet of trawlers after the war, emerging as the premier trawler owners, and also becoming marine engineers, fish salesmen, fish and ice merchants and fish exporters, while Harvey's specialised in shellfish. As fishing declined on the East Coast, those who wished to remain in the industry headed for Newlyn.

Today, seasoned fishermen are still yarning in Newlyn's pubs and at the Fishermen's Mission in the time-honoured way. Ex-Lowestoft trawlerman Jack Garrod, who fished these waters on the mackerel boats from Lowestoft in the 1970s, made his base here in 2002. He explained:

'I could see Lowestoft going down and down. I'd been fishing since I left school at 16 so I had to just jump on a train and go somewhere to continue fishing and try to get a wage. I was on the Stevenson's trawlers, beam trawling. There's a lot of the Lowestoft men living in Newlyn now, and a lot of people come from Grimsby, Hull and all around. Stevenson's are the biggest trawler-owner company at the moment. I've also worked with Stephen Hicks on his boat *Ben McCree*, gill netting.'

I asked what life was like aboard the deep sea trawlers.

'When we was in the North Sea we would be away anywhere between ten to 14 days, but on the Stevenson's trawlers six to eight days. We're a family when we are at sea, living at close quarters. Maybe if you didn't get on with a certain person, he'd have to leave the boat, or you left the boat. You went elsewhere and you carried on.

'The work is very intensive when you're at sea. It might be flat calm to Gale Force 2 to Gale Force 10 … sometimes when you're hauling or shooting the nets you get waves come over the boat, over the side of the rail, push you from one side of the deck to the other. You have to get dried up, put clean clothes on and get straight back out again.'

Ex-Grimsby trawlerman Mick Mahon, known to one and all as 'Grimmie', was strongly critical of our government, perceived by many to be favouring foreign fishermen in our waters: 'Betrayed by our own politicians, who sold British fishermen down the river!' And he recalled a conversation with one of his French counterparts some years ago who joked, 'Every time we have a good trip and return to France, we go to the bar and drink a toast to the British Fisheries Minister!'

Grimmie worked for Stevenson's for a while when he arrived here about 30 years ago, before acquiring his own boats. He spoke of life at sea hauling the nets, taking turns with the watches and snatching periods of sleep in their bunks.

'You normally had a cook, a decking cook, so he'd cook the meals. He'd be on deck as well, but he wouldn't take a watch in the wheelhouse. If you'd got a good cook, you'd

111

eat very well, and you needed to eat well because it's in the nature of the job. You'd normally have two main meals a day, breakfast, and a sort of dinner at teatime.'

When I asked if fish was on the menu, he replied,

'No, no, no. Very seldom fish. I personally don't eat fish at all. I cannot eat fish. No. But you'll have your egg, bacon, beans and jam, toast and all the trimmings. A proper breakfast. And it's a full roast with all the vegetables. Plus during the day and all through the night there's bread and butter and cheese, and various snacks left out.

'In the old days you had coal stoves, then oil stoves. The oil-burning stoves were like old-fashioned Agas. They used to run off the diesel, same as you'd run your engine off.

'While you were at sea you'd gut your fish, and wash them. Then you'd separate them into different varieties, and pass them down to the Fish Room. The Mate was in charge of the Fish Room normally, and when it's landed he's the one who has the responsibility. He then boxes it, and ices it, and stows it away safely till you come into the harbour. Then you'd land your fish. You might be alongside the market, where you can take it straight in, or you might load it onto a lorry on the quay, which brings the fish up to the market. When I first came to Newlyn, Shippam's had a big factory here. They used to buy fish off the market, and make fishpaste.

'Around that time a fishing boat came into Newlyn with some monks aboard. There were about six Irish monks, who were fishing. In the old days the fishermen believed that it was unlucky to encounter somebody in holy cloth around the harbourside, and when that happened old Joe Brownfield, skipper of the *Roseland*, wouldn't go down to the quay.

'When you're out fishing it's fantastic when you get dolphins alongside the boat. Dolphins will come up to your boat and they'll stay with you – then they'll clear off. But if you come out of the wheelhouse and go on deck, bang the side of the boat, or shout, they'll do anything you want. You're interacting with these dolphins, and they'll stay with the boat as long as you stay on deck. They'll come along, swim round and jump out of the water.' And he went on to talk about Beaky, the dolphin who became quite a celebrity in the 1970s. Skipper Stephen Hicks, a fifth generation fisherman brought up in Newlyn also remembered Beaky: 'It was in Newlyn and off the slip at Mousehole as well as in Falmouth. I jumped in the harbour and rode round on its back several times, and it felt like wet velvet. If it went too fast and I started slipping off, it would realise and slow up.'

Stephen went on,

'Our boat the *Karenza*, which means 'my love' in Cornish, she sunk the year after that. She sunk 50 miles north of St Ives and I was the last man to leave her. We had a diesel stove and the diesel leaked. It reached flashpoint and then it blew. Once the boat caught fire there was nothing we could do – obviously we tried to put it out. I went down the ladder and put a fire extinguisher round the corner, pressed the button, and when the end melted I thought it was time to leave …

'You could feel it ablaze, feel the deck trembling. We launched the first life-raft. I asked who couldn't swim and a couple got in the first one. And then when we went to launch the second one, and I went to throw it over the side, this bloke refused to throw it. I asked him why and he said, "I can't swim." I said, "Why didn't you say so and get in the first one?" He said, "I didn't like to"! But we all got in the life-rafts, and then a boat called the *Gamba Bay* came and picked us up. Then the Royal Navy turned up, and they had to sink her because she was a hazard to shipping.'

It seems somewhat paradoxical that so many fishermen are unable to swim, but as Stephen pointed out:

'When you're so far out from land, what are you going to do if you *can* swim?'

'I started fishing in 1973. Years ago it used to be an awful lot of fun, but it's got a very serious business. Before, you'd sort of go along quite happy-go-lucky and enjoy it. There's been millions of colourful characters in Newlyn. We had one called Peter Hitchens. He was master of a schooner. He would crack jokes, but he always told the same stories every week. And he'd laugh so much you'd laugh at him laughing, not at his jokes you'd heard so many times before. But you had to laugh, because he was a very likeable man. His brother was known as Joe Pasties.

'They all had nicknames. In fact, there's some men I don't even know, and never knew, their real names. We had one old man years ago, was called Paws, because he had great big hands. And they played practical jokes. Got up to all sorts of tricks. The favourite one was the tobacco tin. Turn the tin upside down, put the top on the bottom, so when they went to pick the tin up, all the tobacco went on the floor. That was one of the old tricks they used to play.'

Chapter 15

Any Little Cove

Fishing was traditionally carried out from any little cove where boats could be hauled up on the shore, and sometimes mining families did some fishing as well.

Pausing during a break from a friendly game of cards at the Fishermen's Mission in Newlyn, Ronnie Thomas told me,

'I started fishing when I was a young boy in a cove down off the Pendeen Lighthouse. I started with a person called Roland Hill in his little boat, a little 15-ft open boat. He took me out to do a bit of mackerelling and pollacking to see how I got on, and we got on really well together. I fished with him on and off right up until he died, about six or seven years ago. Mackerelling, pollacking, long lining – that was from the shore.

'We would catch anything up to 100 stone, 200 stone in that boat. And then come in and sort it out down on the beach, and bring it to the market in Newlyn. It had to be graded from small, medium and, like, large medium, and large. If you had 200 stone, that would take a good two hours to sort, before you could even come here. There was about eight or ten of us working full time out of the cove at that time, in five boats, two people to a boat. There was a lot of freedom, because you can go to sea when you want to go to sea – if it's fine, you go, if it's a bit lumpy, you wouldn't go.'

Ronnie spoke of the contrasting conditions sometimes encountered on each side of Land's End, and continued his story,

'Then Roland Hill got a 30-footer called the *Silver Spray*, based in Newlyn, which we done netting from. So if we couldn't go out fishing that side of Pendeen because of a groundsea, you could come in here and go out in the bigger boat.

'Well, here in the wintertime we used to do winter mackerelling. And you'd never seen so many boats in your life. There was about 400 and they would come from all over, from Looe, Falmouth, everywhere. That was in the 1970s, 1980s. You would have anything from a 20-ft boat up to a 60-ft boat, all going for mackerel. Looking out there first thing in the morning, just as it was coming daylight, it would be like Piccadilly Circus. The whole bay used to be full. All the lights of the boats … it used to be really good, you know. You wouldn't actually go out and fish at night, but you'd go out in the dark in the morning, to see if you could find your marks. Marks? That's the fish marks that would come up on your meter and tell you were over a shoal of fish. Once you'd found your marks, you'd wait until it started to come light and then you'd start fishing.

'When the mackerel died out, then we started to fish for spur dogs. And as the dogfish got less and less, then we were going deeper. You had your mackerel, and your mackerel run down. Then your dogs come. Caught the dogs, and the dogs would run down. Well then, turned over to the wrecks. Shooting your nets on the wrecks for pollack and ling and all. And then we started searching for something else, which was hake. And now the hake is dying out …

'Years ago, we was out for days looking for a wreck, but we couldn't find one because everyone else had got there before we had. It was getting that we had to do something, and I said, "Well, let's go back and get our dog nets and go looking for dogs." And we spent two more days on top of that steaming up to Lundy Island, and couldn't find anything. We'd had enough by then, but when we got off the back of the Scilly Isles these marks that I'd not seen before come up on the fish meters. So I said, "This gear must go overboard, let's put 'en in here." So we shot them, and when we came back the next day we had 17 hundred stone of hake. And that's how the haking started down here. Nobody else had ever caught them here, not like that. They'd caught the odd hake, but never in *gill* nets. It had never been done before. See, it wasn't like we were looking for hake because we wasn't, we was looking for dogs. That was a really good surprise, because we were getting fed up with looking out on wrecks, when everybody else was there.'

Ronnie told me of a less pleasant surprise with familiar, everyday fishing equipment.

'I have been shooting away lines myself for a long time, and no problem. But I was on the 40-ft *Solitaire*, and I've had a hook slip back into my foot – go right through – and pull me overboard. I've actually gone right under and I've had to catch hold of it – like, rip it out – so I could get back up again. I've shot away thousands and thousands of them and had no problem, but this one just slipped back. As you are shooting the line is coming behind you, really tight, so you haven't time to mess around.'

Chapter 16

St Ives in the Sunshine

In days of yore the harbour at St Ives was a vibrant scene of maritime activity, and it enjoyed close links with foreign and some home ports. Master mariners, pilots, sailors, coastguards, customs men and fishermen thronged the quayside, where shipwrights, anchor smiths, sail makers, rope and net makers plied their trades. Fishwives would be packing fish for export, while 'hobblers' sought to glean a livelihood by turning their hands to anything that needed doing around the harbour, which was filled to capacity with an array of vessels. Some of the fishermen also manned the lifeboat, and carried out many heroic services in the cause of saving life from shipwreck. They were at the heart of the community, and maritime matters were of paramount importance.

Back in 1950 Joe Murrish, the harbourmaster, recalled the days when the place was teeming with fishing boats, providing employment for hundreds of men, with young lads known as 'lappies' being taken on to assist the crew. At that time yachts and motor boats could be seen in the harbour, alongside a few long liners, trawlers and crabbers. A number of fishermen had found

Luggers in St Ives harbour in the 1930s. (Cornish Studies Library)

alternative employment after the Second World War, and others were turning their attention to operating pleasure boats to cater for the increasing number of visitors.

In 1990, when fisherman and budding artist Eric Ward was harbour master and coxswain of the lifeboat, his crew were mainly fishermen. By that time an increasing number of premises near the waterfront were geared to the needs of tourists. Cars had become quite a problem in the steep and narrow streets, and there was a charge for parking on Smeaton's Pier, where fishermen unloaded their catches into pick-up trucks.

Former lifeboatman and fisherman Jack Murt, who described himself as Eric's assistant in the Harbour Office, rather than his deputy, talked about the current state of the fishing industry:

'Well, we're dying off. We've lost a lot of netters and that.

119

We've got a lot of smaller boats on the mackerel and such, and they do a bit of bass netting in the wintertime. There again, you've got a lot of youngsters in these boats that work hard. All sorts of funny hours, midnight, two or three o'clock in the morning. Where other youngsters are lying in their beds, and groaning that they gotta get up at seven, these chaps are out of bed and out working.'

At this point we were joined by others, who indulged in friendly banter, and drew my attention to the customary nicknames. These included Donald-My-Honey, Matthey Fake, Georgie-Trawl, Bob-Cush, John-Ju-Ah, Jan-Perks, and Willie-Pope.

The harbour was bathed in sunshine, the tide was out, and fisherman Robert Yeo was doing maintenance work on his boat, the *Bluebell*, when I met him on Smeaton's Pier in 2009. There were quite a few people enjoying the ambience of the harbourside in the pleasant autumn sunshine, as Robert recalled the idyllic days of his youth.

'It was a lovely childhood here. It was totally unspoilt and we had complete freedom. I was rowing the small boats when I was nine years old. I spent a lot of time with Willie Bish – his proper name was Willie Care; Bish … I think it came about because he couldn't say "dish". There was three brothers, George, John and Willie, and they had a boat. They were fishing all their lives and they had a boat built that sailed from here. She was called the *Lamorna*, and she was caught in a terrible storm and everybody thought they were lost, but they weren't and Willie wrote a little book about it.

'There was about 30 or 40 full-time people here, fishing, then, with a lot bigger boats than there are now. It was mainly long lining. They worked with the tangle nets for crayfish or lobsters, and some of the boats were mackerelling. And that would carry on for, like, the summer season, and then in the winter the boats would go away to Newlyn and some would go around to Looe. Tangle netting,' he explained, 'means that the net is set slack, and the fish or crabs or lobsters go into it, right into the net. Then they're tangled, or tied, up,' and he mimed the process very elegantly as he spoke.

'When I first fished out of here, no boats went to sea on Sundays. None. Not ever. And that lasted till probably around 1960. The first boat, I think to do it was the boat I was working on at that time, the *Cornish Queen*, with Danny Paynter.

'Well, I've fished out of Newlyn for many years. I started trawling in 1980. I started off with a 23-ft small trawler called the *Solea*, and then I bought a Scotch boat which was 33 ft, called the *Lenten Rose*. Then I bought a 40-ft Scotch boat from Padstow, and that was called the *Harvest Reaper*, and then I had a small beam trawler built in Bristol. Then I had a wooden trawler built at Tom's, that's at Polruan. And then I came back home to St Ives, and built my own little boat.

'The older people were definitely better characters. They didn't worry about things. They didn't have a mortgage, most of them lived in council houses or in houses left by the family. Very few had a car. So their life, basically, was fishing and going mainly to the Sloop Inn for a few drinks. There were 20 or 30 fishermen then, and it was just yarns and we had a laugh, and we were singing old Cornish songs. Yeah, life was fun, and laid back. Right, we worked hard, but we didn't worry about things. We all looked after each other, and if somebody had a problem with their boat or whatever, people would help.

'Going back 30 years or so, the Sloop was the fishermen's pub. A lot of the potters and the artists and writers would come to the Sloop, and that was good fun. The fishermen drank in the Front Bar, as they called it. There were two long tables in there, with four long benches. And you could set your clock at what time of day it was when they came in. The majority of them, they had their own places, so they weren't very happy when they walked in and the visitors were sitting in *their* seats. But they had ways and means of sorting things out. Pushing a tankard of beer that way, making some comment or something like that, and they normally got their seats quite quickly! I can remember Gammo, and Wally Andrews, and Jack Wedge, Danny Paynter, William Huss, yeah ... Bendick, Jack Murt, and Peter Coffey. He fished here all his life. And there were three or four of them that used to bring their dogs in, and they were all characters as well. Jack Paynter, he had a boat called the *Osborne Bay*, and he had a dog he called Skipper. It was jet black, and he used to take it to sea. Yeah, a real sea dog.

Old 'Man Friday' Paynter, who used to spin a yarn or two in the Sloop Inn. (St Ives Museum)

'Jack Murt, he always fished with Boko. Boko, his voice was very loud – you could hear it all over the harbour. Boko, that's Richard Knowles. He was a big man, probably about six foot one or six foot two, whereas Jack was much smaller, but they worked together for 20-odd years. They were great characters. Boko, and I think a couple of other people, they started off a Boatmen's Outing, as we called it. That would happen in September or October time, at the end of the season. We would hire a coach, a 52-seater, and it was always full. Depending on where we went we paid a fiver each, or something like that. And it was a good day out. We used to leave about 7 o'clock in the morning and then the coach would leave the last place at closing time – normally we would go to

The Cornish Belle, *in which Dan Paynter took tourists out to Seal Island after the Second World War. (Sheila Bird Collection)*

Plymouth, Looe and Brixham, but only two at a time. Meaning, we would go to Plymouth for the lunchtime session, then go back to Looe, like, for the evening session.

'I remember one time we went to Brixham for the lunchtime session, to the Rising Sun which is right on the front. And there was a character called Ronnie Mitchell, and he was a touter for Dan Paynter, who ran the *Cornish Belle* and the *Cornish Queen*. He came out of the pub slightly worse for wear. But he still had some Seal Island tickets in his coat pocket. The beer funds were getting low so he decided to sell some tickets for Seal Island, and he told the people to go to the end of the quay. The problem was, that they were in Brixham and not in St Ives. But Ronnie, he had his beer money for going to Looe that night!'

Chapter 17

Looking Towards the Future

The fishing industry was always of paramount importance in Cornwall, where fresh or cured fish boiled up with potatoes formed the staple diet throughout the year. Although there had always been bountiful and lean seasons, the traditional pattern of fishing had allowed the fish stocks an opportunity to replenish themselves.

The development of motorised vessels and advances in technology in the latter part of the 19th century began to upset this balance and led to over-fishing in Cornish waters. Some people attributed variations in the movements of fish shoals around these shores to disturbances caused by mechanised fishing boats. Contemporary newspaper reports reflect the concerns of forward-thinking environmentalists in regard to preserving the marine environment and maintaining our fish stocks, and this led to various Acts of Parliament being passed. The arguments have a strangely modern feel to them today.

In September 1890, for instance, the *West Briton* reported that Mr Matthias Dunn (from a well-known Mevagissey fishing family) had read a paper on the 'Decline of Fisheries on the Cornish Coast – its Causes and Cures'. He spoke of the decline of the Cornish summer pilchard and hake fisheries, pointing out that in olden times every fishing village from Plymouth to Land's End had had large pilchard seines, which had been very successful until the last 30 years or so. He attributed the shortage of pilchards, hake, haddock, conger, ling, cod and other species to changes in modes of fishing which had damaged habitats, upset the natural balance and created a knock-on effect along the food chain.

He spoke of the damage done to the seabed by fleets of trawlers, and commended his brother Moses' invention of a device which speared the flat fish without destroying the corals and sponges. He referred to research and practical work carried out by the Armenian government and the Fishery Commission in the United States, and put forward the idea that a fishing craft be fitted out to be manned by practical and scientific men to carry out research around the waters of Great Britain and the west coast of Ireland.

Mr Dunn touched on the subject of localised fishing territory when he mentioned that the Mevagissey Bay area had supported four trawlers of about 15 tons for four months of the year until about 1881, after which increasingly large steam trawlers from Fowey, Falmouth, Plymouth and other areas ventured this way and over-fished their waters.

Would he and other enlightened members of the Cornwall Sea Fisheries' District Committees around the coast have envisaged a time when the fate of the Cornish fishing industry might lie in the hands of bureaucrats from afar?

At the beginning of the 21st century, the media in the West Country carried regular reports of the effects of political goings-on and the plight of our fishermen. All the fishermen I have met in recent years strongly criticised the way successive governments have handled the situation. They talked about the Common

Fisheries Policy allowing Britain's fishing grounds to be flooded by boats from other countries, and of the factory ships from Eastern Europe almost wiping out the fish stocks in the 1970s. They talked of quotas, the dumping of fish and certain regulations which they perceived as being weighted against them. The policy of decommissioning boats, which then have to be broken up, has been condemned as 'legalised vandalism', for it led to the destruction of some fine old wooden craft which were an irreplaceable part of our maritime heritage.

Joe Bussell of Looe put it in a nutshell when he said, 'Ever since we joined the Common Market, the fishing industry has been put down. A lot of politics has entered into fishing. It's killed the fishing industry. It's all gone to hell!'

Writing in the *Western Morning News* in November 2009, recently-retired fisherman Thomas Hay, former chairman of the Fishermen's Association Ltd and one of the country's leading experts on the Common Fisheries Policy, exposed what he believed had really been happening, on the pretext of conserving our fish stocks. He said that the ultimate aim was to create a single EU fleet with 'only a fragment of the once proud and prosperous British fleet' being part of it. After going into great detail about the background of British fishing grounds, British fishing rights and British fish stocks, he said that the Fishermen's Association Ltd in conjunction with 'Save Britain's Fish', 'is firmly convinced that the only possible way of rescuing the industry from this deliberately introduced slaughter is through the restoration of national control – by way of a UK Act of Parliament – over those waters legally under our jurisdiction in accordance with the United Nations Convention on the Law of the Sea 1982'.

He concluded that it is not too late to save our fishing industry, and that 'the option lies in the hands of the fishermen and politicians'. What is certain, and has emerged in every interview I have undertaken, including those in this book, is the passion which this way of life engenders in the men who risk their lives on the sea around the Cornish coast, and their great respect and affection for those who went before.

Index